INTERACTIVE ASSEMBLIES

Sketches by JON WEBSTER
Assemblies by DIANE WALKER

Scripture Union

From Jon
To Pamela, Deborah, Amy, Andrew, Fiona and Oliver, with all my love.

From Diane
To John and Jean, who began the teaching, with love and gratitude.

Scripture Union, 207–209 Queensway, Bletchley, MK2 2EB, England.

First published 1998

ISBN 1 85999 253 6

British Library Cataloguing-in-Publication Data
A catalogue record for this book is available from the British Library.

AUTHORS' NOTE
The authors gratefully acknowledge the permission to use previously published sketches and information about puppet-making from various sources:

The following sketches were previously published in *Together with Children,* pub National Society, Church House, Great Smith Street, London SW1P 3NZ: 'Daniel'; 'Jonah's story'; 'Come home, son!'; 'Open all hours'; 'Fire-walkers'; 'Rocky Road and Sandy Lane'.

The sketches 'RSVP' and 'Open all hours' were originally published in slightly different forms in the books *RSVP* and *Snookered*, pub Moorley's Print and Publishing, 23 Park Road, Ilkeston, Derby, DE7 5DA. At the time of publication, Moorley's still have available a number of Jon's sketches.

'Open all hours' was previously published in *See*, the magazine of the Southwell Diocese and in *Cracking RE*, the Primary magazine from Stapleford House.

'The Saturday night good Samaritan' has previously been published in *Jesus through Art*, a National Gallery publication. Some of the ideas in the puppet-making section were previously used in an article in *Primary English* – now entitled *English 4–11*, pub English Association, University of Leicester, 128 Regents Road, Leicester LE1 7PA.

Whilst every effort has been made to trace previous publication, Jon's material has been widely used, and any omission from this list is regretted.

Cover design by Nick Ward Illustration
Illustrations by Helen Gale

Printed and bound in Great Britain by Ebenezer Baylis & Son Limited, The Trinity Press, Worcester and London.

CONTENTS

INTRODUCTION

Assemblies by Diane Walker 4
Why use drama in the primary school assembly? by Jon Webster 6

SECTION 1: SKETCHES

How to use these drama scripts 7

Old Testament sketches

Shem's story (Noah) 8
Brotherly love (Joseph) 11
Our David (David and Goliath) 16
Naaman's servant girl 19
Jonah's story 23

New Testament sketches

My name is Zacchaeus 28
A gift to warm the Master's heart (The widow's mite) 31
Parables
- Notes about parables 33
- The two sons 34
- The unforgiving rounders player (The unforgiving servant) 36
- The rich tennis star (The rich fool) 39
- The wedding feast 42
- Open all hours (The lost sheep) 44
- The Saturday night good Samaritan (The good Samaritan) 47
- The lost chord (The talents) 51

A donkey for a king 53
The courtyard 56
The centurion's tale 58
First light 61

SECTION 2: PUPPET PLAYS

Using puppets in school 64
Simple puppets to make in the classroom 65

Old Testament puppet plays

Fire-walkers 69
Daniel (The lions' den) 71
Esther 75

New Testament puppet plays

The innkeeper's story 80
Parables
- 'Come home, son!' (The prodigal son) 84
- Rocky Road and Sandy Lane (The two houses) 88
- The sower and the seeds 91

Notes and Bibliography 94
Index – biblical people and stories 95
Index – thematic 95

INTRODUCTION
Assemblies
by Diane Walker

A school has to provide many assemblies each year. A varied and imaginative programme is essential if the assemblies are to be a useful and welcome part of the daily routine. Drama, at a level suitable to the age and ability of the pupils, can be a useful stimulus. It invites exploration of issues in a non-threatening context – issues which can lead into discussion in RE lessons. However, with the ever-increasing demands made on teachers and their time, the actual preparation and rehearsal required for drama is often prohibitive. In addition, people from the local community often go into schools to take assemblies. Teachers and visitors need assembly material which is relevant and challenging but which requires a minimum of preparation, and little or no rehearsal. Jon Webster's scripts offer the advantages of using drama without its time-consuming drawbacks. The shared responsibility of presenting the scripts also removes what many pupils see as drama's threatening exposure of themselves.

Each drama in this book is followed by an assembly outline. Each story can be used in different ways. In the case of some of the longer dramas, it may be possible to use the drama one day and the assembly outline on a subsequent day to follow up the story. There is scope for using the material in class assemblies as well as on those occasions when a class takes assembly for the whole school.

The place of drama in assembly is explored by Jon on page 6. Here are some notes about the assemblies which have been based upon the drama scripts.

Respecting pupil integrity

When conducting an assembly it is vital to respect the position of each pupil. Agreement with ideas expressed in the assembly should never be assumed. Statements of belief should always be introduced with a distancing phrase such as 'Christians believe that...' or 'This is an important belief to Christians...' This is especially important at prayer time. A prayer should be introduced with a phrase such as 'I am now going to say a Christian prayer...' Pupils should not be asked or expected to join in with such prayers, but they should be expected to listen quietly and with respect. The leader can make this plain while introducing the prayer. The chorusing of 'Amen' at the end of prayers is firmly established in many schools, but as this word means 'So be it', signifying the speaker's agreement with the prayers expressed, its repetition should not be demanded. The home situation of individual pupils should always be borne in mind during the assembly, so that pupils are not asked to take part in anything that would compromise or be in opposition to the ethos and beliefs expressed at home. Related to this is the acceptance of any response from the pupils to the material, as long as this response itself is respectful of different interpretations and is appropriately expressed for the occasion.

Contextualising

For an act of worship to be meaningful to pupils, it must relate directly to and be grounded in their everyday lives and experiences. From this base, the content should encourage the pupils to explore the theme in a wider Christian context. A Christian act of worship will show how the theme has been and is of influence in a Christian's life. The notes below on the content show how these assemblies seek to fulfil these aims.

Planning

It is hoped that these assemblies will require the minimum of preparation on the part of the teacher. Most assemblies begin with a section entitled 'You will need', detailing items the leader will need during the assembly, but very few of these require materials not immediately to hand in the classroom.

Introduction

Each assembly has a section entitled 'Introduction'. This, usually, is the part of the assembly which grounds the theme securely in the pupils' own lives and experience. It also acts as the link between the drama and the assembly.

Core material

This section contains the main teaching of the assembly, presenting the theme of the material and exploring its implications.

Prayer/Reflection

Most assemblies end with a prayer or a reflection, and some have a choice of the two. Leaders can decide which is the more appropriate ending to use. When prayers are used, the points above concerning their use should be borne in mind. If the reflections are used, it should be made clear to the pupils that these subjects are for reflection only: they will not be asked to share their thoughts at a later time. Sometimes, questions are given to the pupils during the assemblies for them to consider: again, we do not ask for a verbal response. It is often a good idea to provide some sort of visual focus for the pupils when they are asked to reflect. A lighted candle is ideal for this, as long as strict safety rules are applied. A vase of flowers or simply a picture could also be used.

Music

Suggestions for possible songs relating to the theme are included. These are taken from the following books:

Junior Praise, compiled by P Burt, P Horrobin & G Leavers, pub Marshall Pickering, 1992 (Combined words edition) ISBN 0 551 02639 1
[Music in two books:
Junior Praise Music Edition ISBN 0 551 01293 5,
Junior Praise 2 Music Edition ISBN 0 551 02480 1]

Children's Praise, compiled by G Leavers & P Burt, pub Marshall Pickering, 1991, ISBN 0 551 02423 2
[Out of print since 1995, but still widely used]

The Complete Come and Praise, compiled by G Marshall-Taylor, pub BBC Books, 1990, ISBN 0 563 34580 2
[Music edition ISBN 0 563 34581 0]

A Year of Celebration: Songs for Children, ed J Porter & J McCrimmon, pub McCrimmon Pub Co, 1995, (Pupils edition) ISBN 0 85597 552 0
[Melody edition ISBN 0 85597 544 X]

Background notes

These are not intended to be read to the pupils as they stand. They are intended to provide information for the teacher, who may then select some to use in class.

Indexes

Two indexes are included. One is a straightforward index of biblical characters in the plays and assemblies. The other lists the themes inherent in the assemblies and the biblical material, and is intended to enable teachers to relate the assemblies more easily to their own syllabus.

Health and safety

When leaders and pupils are asked to take part in any activity in the assemblies, health and safety regulations should always be considered. Teachers are referred to their health and safety documents.

Why use *drama* in the *primary* school *assembly*?

by Jon Webster

Story is a very powerful tool for putting across the truth. Jesus was not the first or last teacher to make use of this medium, but he certainly knew how to use it to the best effect. The popularity of stories is attested by the viewing figures for TV 'soaps'.

Drama is a means of getting children actively involved in the storytelling process – they become 'doers', not merely 'hearers' or 'watchers'. As they take this step, their understanding begins to grow. They begin to feel for the characters they are playing as they take on roles and face the problems and dilemmas posed by the plot.

However, for the teacher or presenter, drama can be threatening: what if it gets out of control?

My aim in producing these scripts is to provide a 'user-friendly' approach to beginning drama with pupils. I have tried to build in controls so that you will soon be working with real confidence.

There are a few suggestions for putting the scripts to effective use on page 7. I hope you and your pupils will enjoy using them to share the stories with their audience, and that they will indeed come to a deeper understanding of the meaning of the stories in the process.

SECTION 1: SKETCHES

How to use these drama scripts

by Jon Webster

I've been writing sketches for children and young people for some years, but I've found the main problems have been getting the children to learn and say and act individual parts.

1 Children often *mean* to learn their lines, but never actually get round to doing it.
2 They get very self-conscious when they're on stage and mumble their lines or even whisper them.
3 Self-consciousness also causes them to do tiny actions that no one in the audience can see.

To overcome these problems, I've written these sketches which can be narrated by the teacher or leader of the assembly, but in which the lines are spoken by one or two choruses made up of groups of pupils. In some sketches, there are parts for two narrators.

So how do we use them?

1 We all practise the chorus lines *together*, so that we all learn them. The lines can be displayed on a board or overhead projector at the back of the room during the performance.
2 We all *say* the chorus lines together, so that there shouldn't be any problem for the audience in hearing them.
3 We all *do* the actions together, so that they can be *big* and *expressive*.
4 Individual actors are chosen to step out of the chorus and *mime* the story in front of the chorus, while the chorus are saying the lines and doing their actions behind them.

In these sketches, the chorus members are the real stars!

When a performance has been given, you can even *repeat* it, inviting the audience to join in with the words and actions. In this way the audience is drawn into the storytelling process. The more deeply the pupils are drawn into creating and telling the story, the deeper will be their understanding. So, if time allows, get the pupils to make up their own versions of the stories as short pieces of improvised drama. But don't feel guilty if you don't have the confidence to do this at first.

Use the scripts in the way you feel most comfortable. You know the pupils; use the material in the way that suits you and your group. As your confidence grows, you will probably want to make changes to my scripts and, perhaps, even start to write your own!

Enjoy the drama with the pupils!

Would these pieces be described as plays, sketches or merely 'acted-out-stories'? I don't think it matters!

Have fun!

OLD TESTAMENT SKETCHES

Sketch: SHEM'S STORY

CHARACTERS

NARRATOR (N)
CHORUS 1 (C 1)
CHORUS 2 (C 2)

N: Here's a question for you: if you lived miles from the sea, what's the last thing you'd need to build? Answer: a boat! Let me explain. My name is Shem and I live with my brothers Ham and Japheth – and our wives and families – and my mother and father. You'll have heard of my father – Noah. That's right – the man who built the ark! What's an ark? The boat I told you about a moment ago. But let me begin at the beginning. We lived in cruel times. Lawless times! People fought and stole, told lies and were most unkind to each other. The world was an awful place. Dreadful! But there was one corner of the world that was different and that was our home. You see, my father, Noah, loved God and listened to him, and when God told him to do something, he did it. And that's what made all the difference! You couldn't have met a kinder man than my father. So, while everywhere else was awful, full of suffering and unhappiness, our home was a good, kind, safe place to live in – and all because of my father, Noah, who did as God told him. Well, it couldn't go on like that, could it? God had to do something about the state of things! The world should have been a great place to live, full of happy people – like my family. But it had been spoiled – ruined, in fact. And that made God sad. So, what did he do? He decided to start all over again. A fresh beginning! But then, there was my father, Noah, and us – his family – what would God do about us? Well, as it turned out, God had a part for us in his plan.

C 1: Noah, you must build an ark!

N: I said I'd come to that, didn't I?

C 1: A big wooden boat with plenty of room for you and the family. But you'll need more room than that! I want you to make room for two of every kind of animal and bird on the earth!

N: He even gave us the plans and measurements for the boat. He said...

C 2: Soon, there'll be rain and a great flood. Every living thing will drown, except you and your family and the living creatures on the ark. You will be safe – if you follow my instructions.

N: Now, I told you my father always did what God told him, didn't I? Well, as soon as God gave him the instructions, he set to work to build the ark – and that meant we had to lend a hand as well. Now, you can just imagine what the neighbours thought, can't you? They laughed till their sides split!

C 1: A boat? Here? Miles from the sea?

N: Most men would have given up, but not my father! He just went on building. God had told him what to do, and he was going to do it, no matter what anyone else thought. It was hard work though, but we did it! There was no time to stand back and admire our handiwork – God said the rain would come in seven days, so we had to start getting on board straight away. The animals and birds had to be rounded up – two of every kind, just as God had said.

C 2: And take plenty of food for them all.

N: What a task! My job was counting all the animals in.

C 1: Camels… one, two! Goats… one, two! Sheep… one, two!

N: As they came up the gangplank, I ticked them off on my tally chart. When they were all in, it was time for the family. When we were all aboard, God closed the door with a satisfying bang. We were only just in time! Big black clouds appeared on the horizon and soon great drops of rain were splashing down onto the deck. Lightning flashed and thunder shook the boat. The animals inside were terrified and, I must admit, we were pretty scared, too. Big puddles formed on the dry ground. It poured! Rained cats and dogs it did – if you'll pardon my little joke! But then things got beyond a joke. The puddles grew into lakes. Then the lakes grew into seas. Soon there was one huge sea as far as the eye could see! Water! Everywhere! No houses, no woods, no hills! Even the mountains were rapidly disappearing under the flood! And the ark? By this time we were gently floating across the water. Then we began to understand. The ark had saved us – and all because my father had done what God told him. And the animals – we had saved them, too. Saved from a watery fate! We were all safe and sound. The ark was gently bobbing up and down on the flood. But the rain didn't stop! It went on for forty days – a long, long time! Mind you, there was always plenty to do, feeding all those animals.

Then, one day the rain stopped and the wind began to blow. Slowly, day by day, the water-level went down, till one day there was a terrific BUMP! We had stuck – the ark, I mean – on the top of a mountain – Mount Ararat. But we couldn't get out – we were surrounded by water. Were we ready for some fresh air! Everyone was itching to stretch their legs on solid ground again. Anyway, my father sent out a little bird, a dove. Maybe she would find some solid ground to perch on. But no! All she did was fly round and round and then back to the ark. What a disappointment! Everyone's face fell. Then, a week later, he sent out the little dove again. This time she flew round and round and came back with a leaf in her mouth – not an old brown leaf, but a fresh, green one – newly plucked. This time we were really excited! It wouldn't be long now! Then God spoke to my father again.

C 2: Noah, it's time to go! You can leave the ark now. Off you go, Noah! Everybody out!

N: We opened the door and peered out. Immediately we screwed up our eyes – the sun was so bright! And the water? It had gone! The world looked so beautiful – fresh and green and new. We couldn't wait to go – nor could the animals! The birds sang for joy, and my father just yelled…

C 1: Thank you, Lord!

N: … at the top of his voice. I'll never forget the feel of solid ground under my feet or the smell of the flowers.

C 2: Look up at the sky, Noah!

N: … said God. And there it was – breathtaking – a great arc of beautiful pastel shades – purple, blue, green, yellow, orange and red – a rainbow! We couldn't take our eyes off it. Then God spoke again.

C 1: Noah, I will never send a flood to destroy the world again. The rainbow will remind you and me of this promise.

N: And God keeps his promises. Ask my father, Noah!

Assembly: SHEM'S STORY

THEME: *Obedience*

This play is based on the story of Noah, which can be found in Genesis 6:1 – 9:17.

Introduction

Tell the pupils that you have some new school rules for them to obey today. Make up two or three ridiculous – but harmless – rules, such as:

- Every time you say please today you must touch your left foot.
- You are not allowed to eat any chocolate at all today.
- Only pupils with the letter Q in their names will be allowed to play football at break.

Ask them, how do they feel about these rules? Will they mind having to keep them? Will keeping them do any good? What about the usual school rules: do they think they should keep them? Ask for an example of these, and the reason behind it. Establish the idea that some rules – and obedience to them – are necessary for their own safety and enjoyment of life in school. If necessary, this can be reinforced by talking about other categories of rules, such as those used in football, or those relating to road safety. Add, by the way, those new rules are now cancelled!

Core material

In the play we have just seen, Noah and his family were the only people who were obeying God's rules or laws. God had not given the people silly laws, just to make life annoying and difficult for them. He had given them the laws they needed to live together in safety and happiness. When the people did not obey these laws, trouble started. People were hurt and unhappy, and God's world was spoilt.

Christians believe that the same is true today. God has given his people many laws – but the laws are there to help them, not to make life miserable or difficult. Read out some of the laws below, and ask the pupils to explain why they think these laws are necessary:

- Do not steal from other people.
- Do not tell lies.
- Do not take advantage of people who cannot stand up for themselves.
- Choose people to act as judges. But all of you must act justly and fairly at all times. Do not let yourself be persuaded to act unfairly, or try to make others do so.
- When you buy or sell anything, make sure that the weights and measures are accurate, so that no one is being cheated.

Prayer/Reflection

Help us, Father, to treat other people fairly at all times, and to remember what it feels like to be treated unfairly.

Music suggestions

- Oh, the Lord looked down, 184, *Junior Praise*
- God has promised, 31, *The Complete Come and Praise*

Background notes

- The story of Noah is about judgement – of a corrupt world by a just God. This is a very difficult subject to handle, especially with children. Judgement involves the punishment of the wrongdoer, but it also involves the defence of the victim. People were both the wrongdoers and the victims in this story. Christians believe that God could not allow the mistreatment and spoiling of his world and its people to continue. The emphasis of this story should be on God's care of Noah and his family and his faithfulness in keeping his promises.

- Noah actually sent out a raven from the ark before the dove, but this episode has been omitted for dramatic reasons.

Sketch: BROTHERLY LOVE

CHARACTERS

NARRATOR 1 (N 1)

NARRATOR 2 (N 2)

CHORUS 1 (C 1)

CHORUS 2 (C 2)

N 1: There was once a family of shepherds.

C 1+2: B-a-a!

N 1: Many sons and one old father.

C 1+2: A-a-h!

N 2: So he was called Mr Shepherd ?

N 1: No! His name was Jacob.

N 2: Can I take a family photo? Smile, please!

C 1+2: (*All sulk – arms folded and lips sticking out.*)

N 2: Those sons don't look very happy.

N 1: No, but *he* does! (*Enter Joseph.*)

N 2: Who's he?

N 1: Oh, that's Joseph!

N 2: I like his coat. Very colourful!

C 1+2: Nice!

N 1: That was the trouble! Joseph was his father Jacob's favourite son. He loved him more than he loved all the others.

N 2: Oh, so that's why they all look so grumpy.

N 1: Yes, they were all jealous. But there was more to it than that! You see, Joseph was a dreamer.

C 1+2: Pay attention!

N 1: No, not a *day*dreamer! Joseph had real dreams.

N 2: So, what's wrong with that? We all have dreams, don't we?

N 1: Yes, but Jacob was always telling the others about his dreams. Boasting!

C 1: I had a dream – I was in the fields one day and your sheaves of corn all bowed down to mine.

C 2: Huh!

C 1: Then I had another dream.

C 2: Oh, no!

C 1: The sun and moon and stars all bowed down to me.

C 2: This is too much!

N 1: The brothers had had enough!

N 2: I can see why!

N 1: One day they were in the fields, looking after the sheep.

C 2: B-a-a!

N 2: Was Joseph with them?

N 1: Oh, no – he didn't have to do boring jobs – he just sat around talking to his father all day. Well, father Jacob sent Joseph to find his brothers. It was hot!

C 2: Phew! (*Wipe brows.*)

N 1: Very hot!

C 2: Phew, phew!

N 1: The brothers were in a bad mood – so they plotted to kill Joseph.

N 2: And did they kill him?

C 2: (*Mutter, mutter, mutter.*)

N 1: No, in the end they threw him down a well.

C 1: H-e-l-p!

N 1: Then some traders came by on the way to Egypt...

C 1+2: (*Do Egyptian dance.*)

N 1: … so they sold Joseph to the traders.

N 2: Sold him?

N 1: Yes, the traders would get a good price in Egypt for a fine young slave.

C 1+2: Done! (*Slap hands with each other.*)

N 2: But what did they tell father Jacob?

N 1: They killed a goat and dipped Joseph's beautiful coat in the blood.

C 1+2: U-u-gh!

N 1: Then they told father Jacob that a wild animal…

C 1+2: (*All roar.*)

N 1: … had eaten his favourite son!

N 2: I'll bet Jacob was broken-hearted, wasn't he?

N 1: It nearly killed him!

C 1+2: (*All wail.*)

N 2: A happy family! But what about Joseph?

N 1: I was just coming to him. He was sold to a captain in the king's army.

N 1: He was soon a trusted servant.

N 2: Doing well for himself!

N 1: Yes, until his master's wife told lies about him.

C 1+2: (*All whisper behind their backs and point.*)

N 2: Porky pies, eh?

N 1: Joseph was thrown into prison!

C 1+2: Clang! (*Mime shutting door.*)

N 2: Was he still dreaming?

N 1: In prison he started telling other people, such as the king's butler, what their dreams meant. The butler had a dream and Joseph told him all about it.

N 2: And what did it mean?

N 1: It meant that the butler would soon be set free and go back to serve the king at the palace.

C 1+2: Crystal Palace? Up the Palace! (*Mime waving football scarves.*)

N 1: No, the Royal Palace!

N 2: Any other good dreams?

N 1: No, just bad news! It was the king's baker – he would be leaving prison too.

N 2: That was good news, wasn't it?

N 1: No, the king was going to have the baker killed!

C 1+2: (*All cry, using hankies.*)

N 2: How long was Joseph in prison?

N 1: Two more years. Then the king had a dream, too.

C 1+2: (*All snore.*)

N 1: Seven thin cows will eat up seven fat cows.

C 1+2: (*All snore.*)

N 2: Strange – I thought cows only ate grass.

C 1+2: S-s-s-h! (*Then all snore.*)

N 1: Then seven thin ears of corn will eat up seven fat ears of corn.

C 1+2: (*All snore.*)

N 2: Weird!

C 1+2: S-s-s-sh!

N 1: The king was puzzled.

C 1+2: (*All scratch heads.*)

N 1: What did it all mean? No one knew – not even the king's wisest men!

C 1+2: (*All stroke beards, scratch heads, shake heads.*)

N 1: Then the butler remembered that Joseph was good at dreams. The king sent for him.

C 1+2: (*All snap fingers and beckon.*) Come!

N 1: Joseph listened to the king's dream and asked God's help.

C 1+2: (*All clasp hands as in prayer.*)

N 1: There will be seven years of bumper harvests.

C 1+2: Yippee!

N 1: Then there will be seven years when no food will grow.

C 1+2: Rumble! (*All rub tummies.*)

N 1: No! Don't worry! No one's going to starve to death! You see, God gave Joseph this brilliant plan to save food in the seven good years, ready for the bad years when nothing would grow.

C 1+2: Who's a clever boy?

N 1: The king made Joseph his chief minister...

C 1+2: The boss!

N 1: ... with a ring.

C 1+2: Dring, dring. Hello?

N 1: No, a royal ring for his finger. Joseph's job was to save corn ready for the bad years so that no one would go hungry.

N 2: Hold on, it's almost as if God sent Joseph to Egypt to save everyone from starving!

C 1+2: (*All clap.*)

N 2: Thank you! This *is* a long story, isn't it? But how were the brothers getting on – and father Jacob?

N 1: They were hungry! But they knew where they could buy food.

N 2: Egypt?

C 1+2: (*All clap again.*)

N 1: So Jacob sent the brothers to Egypt to buy corn.

N 2: And they met Joseph and they all lived...

C 1+2: ... happily ever after!

N 1: Not yet! Joseph recognised his brothers, but they didn't recognise him, so they just bowed to him.

C 1+2: (*All bow.*)

N 2: And he sold them the corn?

N 1: Yes, but he wanted to know if they were still jealous men, so he asked them to come back with his younger brother Benjamin – he was Jacob's favourite now. Then he would sell them corn.

N 2: Were the brothers worried?

C 1+2: (*All bite nails.*)

N 1: Yes, but they were also very hungry so they just had to go back and bring Benjamin.

N 2: And Joseph told them who he was and they all lived...

C 1+2: ... happily ever after.

N 1: Not yet! He sold them corn and hid his silver cup in Benjamin's sack of corn.

N 2: Why did he do that?

N 2: It was a sort of test – to see if the brothers had changed. Watch this! The brothers set off for home, but they were stopped by Joseph's soldiers.

C 1+2: Halt!

N 1: The soldiers searched the sacks of corn and...

C 1+2: Abracadabra!

N 1: ... his cup was in Benjamin's sack! Joseph pretended to be angry.

C 1+2: G-r-r-r!

N 1: He ordered the soldiers to throw little Benjamin into prison. But the brothers said...

C 2: No! It would break our father's heart to lose Benjamin. Put us in prison in his place!

N 1: Then Joseph could see that they had changed. They loved their father – and Benjamin. Joseph said...

C 1: It's me – your long-lost brother Joseph!

N 2: And they all lived happily ever after? At last!

N 1: Jacob came to live in Egypt with his long-lost son!

C 1: Three cheers for Joseph!

C 2: Hip, hip hooray! (*Three times.*)

N 2: So God saved *all* their lives through Joseph. A long story!

N 1: Yes, but worth it in the end, don't you agree?

C 1+2: Yes!

Assembly: BROTHERLY LOVE

THEME: *God's perfect planning*

This play is based on the story of Joseph, which can be found in Genesis 37:1–36 and 39:1 – 46:7.

You will need:
a selection of diaries, calendars, planners; sheet of paper divided into columns for the next seven days; two sheets of paper to use as diaries of Joseph's future – one headed 'Joseph's plans for the future' and the other headed 'God's plans for Joseph's future'.

Introduction

Ask if any of the pupils keep a diary. Talk about the uses of a diary – to record happenings day by day, and to make notes about future events, appointments, birthdays, etc. Show them the range of diaries and calendars, perhaps reading out (real or imaginary) examples of these two uses. Use the sheet of paper to plan your next week – either your real intentions or plausible fictional ones. Explain that some people like to have their future planned down to the last detail, and hate surprises and events which alter their plans. There is a famous saying from a poem by a Scottish poet, Robert Burns, which says,

'The best laid schemes o' mice an' men
Gang aft a-gley.'

(This can be paraphrased as: 'the best thought out plans of mice and men often go wrong'.) Talk about its meaning: how might the plans of a mouse be spoilt? Sometimes people's plans are spoilt just as dangerously as the plans of mice!

Core material

What plans do they think Joseph might have made in his diary when he was living at home with his brothers and father? Write down suitable suggestions on his sheet of paper. How would he feel about his life and his future? But the future did not work out as he expected at all! On the other sheet of paper, write down all the unpleasant and dangerous things they can remember that God had already planned for Joseph's future. It seemed that his future was completely spoilt. Draw a thick line under these things, and then ask for the good things that God had planned for Joseph's future. Write these underneath. God knew what he was doing all the time. He wanted Joseph to be in Egypt, in a position of power, so that he was ready to help his family and to save them from starvation during the famine. There were other good things God had planned, too. Add these as you talk about them. During all of this, Joseph himself also learned more about God and about trusting in him. The brothers learned how important their family was to them and were sorry for what they had done to Joseph.

Christians still believe that what Joseph learned was true. God is in control of their lives, even when things seem to be going badly and their own plans are destroyed. They believe that God knows best what they need, and that they can trust him to work everything out for them. His plans are never destroyed by events or people.

Prayer/Reflection

Thank you, Father, that you are in control, whatever plans we might make. Help us to remember, as we make our own plans, that you are planning our futures too, and that you love us.

Music suggestions

- God is working his purpose out, 57, *Junior Praise*
- Thank you, Lord, 32, *The Complete Come and Praise*

Background notes

- Joseph and his younger brother Benjamin were Jacob's favourites, as they were the only two sons of his favourite wife, Rachel.

- The special coat Jacob gave to Joseph might have been multi-coloured: the word used could also mean long-sleeved or white. If so, it would not have been a coat to work in – a further sign of Jacob's favouritism. It was a type of coat usually given to the eldest son, as a sign of his higher status. Joseph was one of the youngest, and should have been of low status. The idea of his family bowing to him would have been insulting in their society.
- The traders were probably Ishmaelites or Midianites, regular traders throughout the Middle East. Joseph was sold for 20 pieces of silver – the price of a male slave. The price was fixed later at 30 pieces – the price paid for Jesus when he was betrayed.
- Egypt's great fertility was entirely dependent on the yearly flooding of the River Nile. If it failed, the country was plunged into famine conditions. Other peoples were often allowed to camp within Egypt during famines. This one was particularly severe, affecting both Israel and Egypt.
- The cupbearer was the Pharaoh's wine taster.
- Dreams were seen as being important predictions of the future. Rulers employed people experienced in their interpretation. The difference here is that Joseph had God's knowledge of the meaning of dreams to help him in their interpretation, and openly acknowledged this.
- Jacob was not unusual at the time in having more than one wife. The pattern of one partner became established later for God's people.

Sketch: OUR DAVID

CHARACTERS

NARRATOR (N) *The narrator in this sketch is one of David's brothers.*

CHORUS 1 (C 1)

CHORUS 2 (C 2)

N: I'll never forget the time Samuel came to our home – Samuel, the great prophet of God from Shiloh. At our little farm! He asked my father…

C 1: Where are your sons, Jesse? Line them up then!

N: We lined up. Then, slowly, he walked down the line – me and my brothers – and paused, in turn, in front of each of us, studying our faces. He seemed to be looking for something – or was it listening? When he got to the end of the line he stopped, puzzled, and asked…

C 1: Have you any other sons, Jesse?

C 2: Only David, but he's just a lad!

C 1: Where is he?

C 2: Up in the hills, looking after the sheep.

C 1: Then send for him!

N: And guess who had to fetch him? Me, of course! My legs were aching and I was out of breath before I found him – sitting on a rock, playing his harp. He could play a good tune, though I say it myself! So David went down the mountainside to meet Samuel – and me, I had to stay and guard the sheep! What did Samuel do when he saw David? Well, according to my brothers, he took out some olive oil and put some on David's head in a ceremony called anointing, which showed David is a person specially chosen by God, like priests and the king.

C 1: The Lord's anointed!

N: Then Samuel went back to Shiloh, leaving all of us very puzzled. What had it all been about? We couldn't work it out! It must mean David was special. But what use was that to us – he was a good shepherd and that was all that counted on the farm. Life went on much as usual – David guarded the sheep and spent the long hours on the hillside practising with his sling and stones – he was a good shot, our David! Then came the war. We became soldiers – me and my brothers, fighting in King Saul's army. Our enemies were the Philistines. The food was awful! But, even worse was…

C 2: … Goliath!

N: Every day a giant Philistine would come over the hill and shout…

C 1: Who will fight me?

N: He was huge! And ugly!

C 1: Israelites, send out a champion to fight me!

N: And did anyone go? Not likely! We knew he could make mincemeat of any of us. Then he'd disappear back over the hill.

C 1: Cowards!

N: This happened every day. No battle could take place until someone took up Goliath's challenge. And no one would, not even King Saul! So every day we sat in our tents, feeling more and more fed up and thinking of home and our mother's cooking. Until the day David arrived to deliver some food from our mother. We soon polished that off!

C 2: M-m-m!

N: David asked us why there was no battle taking place and we told him about Goliath, the giant Philistine. Then, of all things, David jumped up! He said that if no one else would fight Goliath, he would! We couldn't believe our ears. Our little David fight that giant?

C 2: Don't be crazy!

N: But he wouldn't calm down.

C 1: If God is with me, I can beat Goliath!

N: So we took him to King Saul. Saul just laughed at David.

C 2: Don't be crazy!

N: But there was something special about our little brother – he had total trust in God.

C 1: If God is with me, I can beat Goliath!

N: So Saul decided to lend David his armour. He said...

C 2: Put on my breastplate!

N: But that meant David couldn't breathe. Then Saul said...

C 2: Try my helmet!

N: David couldn't lift his head with that on. Then Saul said...

C 2: Here are my shin-guards!

N: But that meant David couldn't pick his feet up. Finally, Saul said...

C 2: Here's my sword!

N: David couldn't even lift it! Then David said...

C 1: If God is on my side, I can beat Goliath!

N: Then Goliath came over the hill and when he saw David, he burst out laughing. Not a friendly laugh, though. It sent shivers down your spine! Then he got angry – what an insult to sent a boy out to fight him, Goliath!

C 2: What's that stick for? Do you think I'm a dog?

C 1: You've got lots of armour. I've got God to help me and we will win!

N: Goliath drew his sword and began to run at David.

C 2: Ch-a-r-ge!

N: David calmly picked up a stone from the stream and put it in his sling. He faced Goliath and waited. If he let fly too early, the stone would fall short. If he waited too long, Goliath would be on top of him. We held our breath and watched – our hearts almost stopped. Then, at just the right moment, David swung his sling and let fly with the stone.

C 1: Ping!

N: The stone hit Goliath between the eyes, and down he went!

C 2: C-r-a-sh!

N: It was all over – for Goliath. Then we all drew our swords. The battle could begin!

C 1: Ch-a-r-ge!

N: Young David's total trust in God had put new heart into all of us.

C 1+2: For the God of Israel!

Assembly: OUR DAVID

THEME: *Trust and David's trust in God*

This play is based on the story of David and Goliath, which can be found in 1 Samuel 17:1–58.

Introduction

James was a good swimmer. He was 14 now, and he had just passed his bronze life-saving badge. Last Saturday, he had swum a mile in a sponsored swim to raise money for a local charity. But today, he was swimming for fun, at the local pool with his father and his younger sister and brother, Louise and Darren. The huge inflatable octopus was in the pool, and he and Darren had been climbing on it. Now, Darren wanted to go to the toilet, so the two brothers swam over to the shallow end, where their father was patiently encouraging Louise to take her feet off the bottom of the pool for the first time, holding her safely while she tried. 'You stay with Louise,' he said, 'and I'll go with Darren.'

Louise was annoyed. 'Hurry back, Dad!' she said. 'I want to try again. I'm sure I'll do it next time.'

'I can help you,' James told her. 'Let's try now before Dad comes back. You can surprise him then!'

But his sister shook her head. 'No, I don't want to.'

James was upset. 'You'll be safe with me!' he said. 'I'm an even better swimmer than Dad!'

But Louise still refused, and she clung onto the side until her father returned. When Louise was in bed that night, James told his father.

'Don't be upset by it,' his dad said. 'I know she would have been safe with you. But she just didn't trust you enough to let go of the side.'

Core material

James was a good swimmer. Louise knew this. He could have kept Louise safe. But she didn't trust him enough to try. What does 'trust' mean? Discuss its meaning with the pupils, pointing out that knowing someone is trustworthy is not the same as actually trusting them. It was like this when the Israelites faced the Philistines and Goliath. The Israelites all knew that God was very powerful, powerful enough to look after them. But none of them trusted him enough to put this to the test. They did not dare to fight Goliath because they did not trust God to look after them. David did trust God. He believed that God would look after him whatever happened, so he volunteered to fight Goliath. He made sure that everyone – the Israelites and Goliath – knew that it was God who would help him to win, not his own strength or skill. But God could only help him because he trusted him enough to try.

Prayer/Reflection

As we grow up, we have to learn whom we can trust. Christians believe that God can always be trusted, and that he will never let them down.

Music suggestions

- God takes good care of me, 46, *Children's Praise*
- Sometimes problems, 461, *Junior Praise*; 154, *Children's Praise*
- Only a boy called David, 190, *Junior Praise*

Background notes

- Samuel actually told the brothers to pass before him, but in the play he walks along their line for dramatic reasons.
- David had worked as a shepherd for his father. The sling was a shepherd's weapon, consisting of a leather strip. A small, round stone would be placed in its middle, and it would be spun around until the stone could be released at great speed. A skilled person could produce stone-speeds comparable to the speed of a world-class fast bowler.
- Saul had the first full-time army in Israel. This consisted mainly of lightly-armed foot soldiers. Only the very rich – like Saul – would have full body armour. David was still a youth and not fully grown; the Bible describes Saul as being taller than his fellows.
- The Philistines lived in and around five cities on Israel's coast. They began a major offensive against Israel in Saul's reign, and this continued, with temporary victories for the Israelites, for many years.

Sketch: NAAMAN'S SERVANT GIRL

CHARACTERS

NARRATOR (N)

CHORUS 1 (C 1)

CHORUS 2 (C 2)

N: I was only a child when the soldiers came to our village. I can't remember much – just shouting and screaming and big men with swords. Then they left and took me with them. Taken from my parents by the Syrians. Made to walk for mile after mile through villages I'd never seen before, across the desert and into a strange land where the people spoke words I didn't understand. I was terrified. I knew I would never see my home or family again. All the dear things of home were gone for ever! I was surrounded by strangers. They took me to Syria. They sold me to a man called Naaman and his wife. Naaman is a good master – a general in the Syrian king's army. He's kind, and so is his wife. They're good people, and although I still miss my family, in a strange sort of way, I've grown to love my master and mistress. They've been good to me, and a time came when I could repay their kindness. I can remember it now. The day the bad news spread. Everyone in the house was weeping – the family, the servants, everyone!

C 1: Have you heard the dreadful news?

C 2: What's wrong?

C 1: It's the master – he's got leprosy!

C 2: Leprosy? What's that?

C 1: Don't you know what leprosy is?

C 2: No!

C 1: Oh, it's a dreadful disease! It starts with marks on your skin, and then it spreads. Soon you can't feel your fingers and toes, and sometimes you go blind!

C 2: I've never seen anyone like that.

C 1: No, that's because people with leprosy have to go and live on their own. No one wants to go near them. They end up as beggars, and that's what'll happen to the master!

N: I was shocked. No wonder my mistress was weeping! My poor master! He didn't deserve this. Then I had an idea! I remembered something I'd heard long ago in my own country, in Israel. I went to my mistress and spoke quietly to her – her eyes were filled with tears. I said…

C 2: Madam? In my country – in Israel – there is a prophet called Elisha. I'm sure he could make my master well!

N: She looked at me, hardly daring to believe.

C 1: Do you really think he could?

C 2: I'm sure he could, Madam!

N: And that's how it all started. My mistress told her husband, and Naaman told the king, and he wrote to the King of Israel…

C 2: My general, Naaman, has leprosy. He must be cured.

N: A bit threatening, I suppose. No wonder the King of Israel was upset when he got it! A bit scared, too, I shouldn't wonder.

C 1: A cure for someone with leprosy? How can I do that? Does he think I'm God?

N: But, somehow Elisha heard about the letter. You know – Elisha the prophet – the one who, with God's help, heals people!

C 2: Send Naaman to me!

N: … he told the king, and they did. My master drove up to Elisha's door in his chariot. They knocked, but Elisha didn't answer it – he sent his servant instead.

C 1: My master says you're to go to the River Jordan, and bathe in it seven times. Then you'll be cured!

N: Now, my master, Naaman, is a good man, a kind man. But now he was angry – very angry! I suppose he felt insulted that Elisha hadn't come out to see him.

C 2: There are finer rivers than the Jordan in my own country, Syria!

N: … he shouted.

C 2: Why should I bathe in this dirty old river?

N: He was all set to come straight home.

C 1: Master, we've come a long way! Do as the prophet says – it's really a very small thing to do – bathe in the river, seven times.

C 2: Oh, very well! I'll give it a try!

N: He did. And it worked! He was cured! When he stepped out of the river Jordan, the marks on his skin were gone. It was perfectly healthy!

C 1: Now I know there is no God but the God of Israel!

N: And he called on Elisha the prophet to thank him. You can imagine the rejoicing when he got home! My mistress was weeping again, but this time her tears were tears of joy. Everyone was happy! And I was happy, too. In some small way I had been able to thank Naaman for his kindness. Thank God!

Assembly: NAAMAN'S SERVANT GIRL

THEME: *Pride*

This play is based on the story of Naaman, which can be found in 2 Kings 5:1–19.

You will need:

sheet of paper and felt-tip pens

Introduction

Ask the pupils what the matter was with Naaman. Discuss what the disease of leprosy meant in those days, using the background information as appropriate. No wonder the family was upset, and no wonder everyone wanted to see Naaman cured! He must have been a good man in many ways. The slave girl who lived in his house and worked for his wife cared about him, even though he was the enemy of her people. His king cared about him and valued his work in his army so much that he was ready to send rich gifts to an enemy king to try to get Naaman cured. But there was something else the matter with Naaman, something else that needed to be cured. Do any of the pupils know what it was?

Core material

Listen to these sentences: 'Oh, she won't like it – she always has her nose stuck up in the air' (or 'She's really stuck up') and 'He really looks down on us just because our car is ten years old'. What do these mean? Does it mean the woman really walks round with her nose pointing upwards like this? (*Demonstrate*.) Or that she is covered with sellotape? Does the other saying mean the man is taller than other people? Discuss what sort of people this man and woman are. This is what was the matter with Naaman. He was vain. He knew how popular he was and how important he was to the king. He had begun to think he was so important that everyone must know about him, and that they should all treat him with great honour. After all, they were lucky to meet him! Now, it is right to feel proud of ourselves when we have worked hard or helped someone, but Naaman wasn't just proud any longer. He was vain, sure that he was very important. So when Elisha didn't even come out of his house to greet him, but just sent a message, Naaman was furious! He had expected the king himself to help him – and now one of the king's servants couldn't even come out to meet him! And, to make it even worse, this servant ordered him to bathe seven times in the smelly old River Jordan! There were much nicer rivers in his own country. Naaman was insulted; his vanity was hurt. He refused. It wasn't until he agreed to bathe in the river, and to ignore his vanity that he was cured – and then he was cured of his leprosy and his vanity at the same time! He realised then that he owed all of this to God and to Elisha, and he went to say thank you to them both.

Other people had thought that the only thing wrong with Naaman was his leprosy. But God knew there was something else wrong with Naaman as well, and God wanted to cure both things at the same time, so that Naaman could be really happy once more.

Christians believe that God knows all about them. He knows the things other people know about them, but he also knows the things that they try to hide from other people as well. They believe that God loves them no matter what they have done, and that he wants to make them well in every way, just as he wanted to make Naaman well.

Prayer/Reflection

Naaman had an obvious illness that made his body unwell. He also had something wrong with him that made his character 'unwell' or unattractive to other people. Ask the pupils for other things like this, for instance temper. Write these on the sheet of paper. Then ask the pupils to think in silence about these and to ask themselves, 'Do I have any of these?' Read the prayer if appropriate:

Father, thank you that you still want to make us completely well in every way. Help us to see if we are doing wrong things, and to ask you to help us stop them.

Music suggestions

- You can't stop rain, 297, *Junior Praise*
- In our work and in our play, 108, *Junior Praise*

Background notes

- Syria and Israel were frequently at war, and border raids were common.
- Leprosy is still a devastating disease, but it is now curable. We now know it cannot be passed on easily by contact, but in biblical times, sufferers were isolated, living difficult, lonely lives away from their families. Several skin diseases were known as leprosy then, and there are various types of leprosy itself: we cannot be sure which Naaman suffered from.
- Naaman suffered from excessive pride, which was hurt by Elisha's casual reception of him, and by the degrading task he had to perform. Bathing in the Jordan was not heroic enough for Naaman. If he had been given a dangerous task, he could have boasted that his cure, at least partly, had been due to himself.

Sketch: JONAH'S STORY

There are a few individual parts in this sketch.

CHARACTERS	**MIMERS**
NARRATOR 1 (N 1)	CAPTAIN
NARRATOR 2 (N 2)	SAILORS
GOD'S VOICE	NINEVITES
CHORUS (C)	PLANT (*dressed in green*)
KING WORM (*dressed in brown*)	
DIRECTOR	
JONAH	

N 1: Once upon a time…

N 2: I've heard this story before!

N 1: No, you haven't!

N 2: Well the one I heard started that way, too.

C: Oooooh!

N 1: Look, just pipe down and let me get on with it!

N 2: Oh, all right.

N 1: Once upon a time…

N 2: When?

N 1: (*Getting really irritated.*) A long time ago! There was a young man called Jonah – an ordinary sort of chap. Well, one day Jonah got an important message from God.

C: Dring, dring! It's for you-hoo!

GOD'S VOICE: Listen, Jonah, I have a job for you. I dare say you've read about the people of Nineveh in the Sunday papers – how unkind they are to each other, and what selfish lives they lead. Now, you know, Jonah, I just can't bear to see that kind of thing going on! So I want you to go to Nineveh and tell them to give up their evil ways. Yes, they must be sorry and change their lives for the better, or I shall destroy their city… with them in it! Is that clear, Jonah? Go to Nineveh! (*Telephone goes dead.*)

C: Who is that? Who's speaking? Oh, he's rung off! And I suppose I do know who it was!

N 2: So did he go to Nineveh?

N 1: Well, what would you do?

N 2: I'd run a thousand miles.

N 1: Correct! That's exactly what he did.

N 2: What? Run a thousand miles?

N 1: Well, not exactly. Actually he got on a boat and sailed a thousand miles.

C: (*Sing.*) I am sailing, I am sailing… (*Swaying.*)

N 2: Where was he going?

N 1: Tarshish – in Spain.

N 2: Really?

N 1: Well, no, not really!

N 2: What do you mean?

N 1: Well, he never got there.

N 2: Why?

N 1: Because he got thrown overboard.

N 2: Got thrown overboard? What kind of a captain would throw a passenger overboard?

N 1: Well, this one did!

N 2: Why?

N 1: Because the ship was in trouble. It was caught in a storm!

C: Rumble, rumble, crash, crash, splash, splash! (*Jonah puts up an umbrella and is blown around the stage, then sits looking seasick.*)

N 2: But why did the captain throw him overboard?

N 1: Well, Jonah said the storm was sent by God – it was all because of him!

N 2: Eh?

N 1: God had sent the storm because he – Jonah – had been disobedient. He hadn't taken God's message to Nineveh!

C: Naughty boy. (*Wag fingers.*)

N 1: The captain didn't want to throw him overboard…

C: All hands on deck!

N 1: But Jonah said it was the only way to stop the storm… and hopped over the side, with the captain's help.

C: (*Holding noses.*) Hold your doses! Splash!

N 2: And the storm died down? (*Jonah mimes swimming.*)

N 1: M-m-m! As flat as a millpond!

N 2: And Jonah?

N 1: He was swallowed by a big fish.

DIRECTOR: Er, Jonah, can you just hide behind the stage for a couple of minutes to give the audience the idea you've been swallowed by a big fish?

N 1: Thanks! Now where did we get to? Oh, yes, Jonah was swallowed by a huge fish.

C: Gulp! Yummy, yummy, yummy!

N 2: Is that it then? Can we all go home?

N 1: What do you mean?

N 2: Well, that's the end of the story, isn't it? It's curtains for Jonah, isn't it?

JONAH: (*Offstage.*) I'm OK. but it's jolly dark in here. Anyone got a light?

N 1: Sssssh! Inside the fish Jonah prayed to God.

JONAH: He-e-lp!

N 1: And God heard his prayer. After three days and three nights inside the fish, it just spewed him up!

N 2: Ugh!

DIRECTOR: Hold it! You can come out now, Jonah!

N 1: Jonah was really glad to be out in the fresh air again.

C: (*Deep breathing.*)

N 1: Then he got another message from God.

GOD'S VOICE: Dear Jonah, go straight to Nineveh and tell the people there to repent of their wicked ways. Say they have forty days to change their lives!

N 2: And did he go this time?

N 1: Yes, it was a long, hot journey. (*Jonah staggers around.*)

N 1: Now, Nineveh was a big city. But Jonah stood up on an old milk crate and told the people to give up their wicked, selfish ways. (*All gather round him.*)

N 2: They didn't repent, of course?

N 1: Now that's where you're wrong! The King of Nineveh got up and said…

KING: Put on sackcloth! Put ashes on your heads! And change your evil ways!

N 1: And they did!

N 2: You don't say?

N 1: I certainly do! They did change their wicked ways. But, wait for it…

N 2: What?

N 1: Jonah wasn't very pleased!

N 2: Eh?

N 1: He said it made him look rather silly.

C: Silly billy!

N 1: So off he went into the desert to sulk. He said he'd known all along that God wouldn't destroy the city.

N 2: I say, I say, I say, what's green and sits in the corner?

C: The Incredible Sulk!

JONAH: I knew all along God would never destroy the people of Nineveh – he's too kind!

N 1: Well, he got pretty hot sitting in the sun!

C: Phew! (*All mop brows.*)

N 1: In fact, the heat made him ill.

JONAH: (*Jonah groans and holds head.*)

N 1: Then a little plant grew up to give him shade.

(*PLANT 'grows' behind Jonah.*)

C: A-a-a-ah!

N 1: Then a nasty worm came along and ate through the little plant.

(*WORM chops down plant – Jonah looks angry.*)

GOD'S VOICE: There you are, Jonah! (*Jonah looks round puzzled.*) You felt sorry for the little plant – but only because it gave you shade. (*Jonah nods.*) Well, I felt sorry for the people of Nineveh – I made them!

N 2: Just a moment! Jonah was a strange sort of a chap, wasn't he? I mean, God gives him a special job to do – stopping a terrible tragedy – and he's sorry when he's successful. Most peculiar! I mean, if God gave me a message to deliver, I'd jump at the chance!

N 1: Really?

TELEPHONE RINGS

N 1: Hello? (*Turns to* **N 2**.) It's for you!

N 2: (*Jumps up.*) Excuse me – must dash! I've got to see a man about a dog!

Assembly: JONAH'S STORY

THEME: *God's mercy is universal*

This play is based on the Book of Jonah.

Introduction

Ask the pupils the following questions: Where would you take a car that wasn't running correctly? Who would you call if the television broke down? Where would you go to buy the meat for dinner or the vegetables? Would you expect all these people to know what to do and to help you? What if the garage worker said, 'Sorry, I don't mend cars'? The television repair man might say, 'I won't mend your television!' What if the butcher's shop and the greengrocer both said, 'Oh no, we don't sell food to people like you!' Would you be surprised? We expect people to be willing to do their jobs when we need them. That's what they're there for.

Core material

Jonah was like a garage owner who refused to mend a car. God asked him to deliver a message to the people of the city of Nineveh. There were two very good reasons why Jonah should do this. God had chosen him to be a prophet. A prophet is a person chosen by God to take his messages to other people. But Jonah should have done this job for another reason, too. Jonah was a Jew, and the Jewish people had been chosen by God as his special people. He had looked after them for many hundreds of years, and he had given them special rules and laws to show them how to live in happiness and safety. The Jews all had a job. They were to show other people how God's people should live, so that when people saw them, they would also see that God was a good God who cared for his people. But at this time, many Jews had forgotten this special job. They just remembered that they were special, and forgot the bit about showing other people what God was like. Jonah was like this. When God asked him to tell the people of Nineveh that they had angered and upset God by the way they behaved, and to tell them what God wanted them to do, Jonah thought, 'No! Why should I tell them about God? They aren't Jews – there's nothing special about them! I don't want them to become God's friends. They've done wrong things – let them suffer for it!'

So God had to send some messages to Jonah himself. He had to show him that he couldn't run away from God, because God is everywhere. Jonah had to learn that God is so powerful that he can do anything he wants. But most importantly, Jonah had to learn that God loves everyone he has made – and that included the people of Nineveh. They had done many wrong things, but God still loved them and wanted to forgive them. It wasn't just the Jews God loved, even though they were his special people. So the messenger had to learn some new messages for himself!

Prayer/Reflection

It is easy to feel that we are better than other people, because of what we've got or because of what we can do. If you feel like this at times, perhaps you can think of a way to share instead.

Music suggestions

- You can't stop God from loving you, 297, *Junior Praise 2*; 102, *The Complete Come and Praise*
- Far beyond the universe, 21, *Children's Praise*
- He's got the whole world, 78, *Junior Praise*; 22, *A Year of Celebration*

Background notes

- The book of Jonah is interpreted in many different ways – as allegory, myth, parable or history. There are modern incidents of people surviving after being swallowed by large sea creatures, so the story should not be viewed as unbelievable. Most Christians agree that its purpose is to teach about God's omnipresence and universal mercy.

- Nineveh was the capital of the Assyrian Empire, known for its cruelty. Jonah might well have been afraid to go there, but his main reason for not going was that he did not want to risk the Assyrians being forgiven by God. He did not want to share the relationship he had with God. He must have been desperate to embark on such a long sea voyage – probably to Spain – as the Israelites were not sailors.
- We do not know what the fish was – the same Hebrew word is used for all sizes of fish, with a qualifying word such as 'great'. All modern versions of the Bible call it a big fish. The writer would not distinguish between mammals and fish: sperm whales or sharks are possibilities in the Eastern Mediterranean. Christians believe the point is that the fish was under God's control and was used by him, and that God is present everywhere – even in the fish!
- The people of Nineveh dressed in sackcloth and put ashes on their heads as a sign of their sorrow for what they had done. Some Christians still use ashes as a sign of repentance on Ash Wednesday at the beginning of Lent.
- This story is read by Jews today on the Day of Atonement to remind themselves of how eager God is to forgive instead of judge.

NEW TESTAMENT SKETCHES

Sketch: MY NAME IS ZACCHAEUS

CHARACTERS

NARRATOR (ZACCHAEUS) (N)

CHORUS 1 (C 1)

CHORUS 2 (C 2)

N: I was once the poorest man in the world. And yet I had everything that money could buy. Puzzled? I'll explain. My name is Zacchaeus and I was a tax collector – for the Romans! Everyone hated me! It stands to reason really, doesn't it? I mean, I worked for the Romans, and everyone hated them.

C 1: Why should we pay taxes to the Roman emperor?

C 2: What has he ever done for us – except take away our freedom!

N: Yes, they hated the Romans. And they hated me – I worked for the Romans, so I was a…

C 1: ... traitor!

C 2: You betray your own people!

N: But there was more to it than that. They hated me for another reason – I was a tax collector – and a cheat! It worked like this: if a man owed the Romans one denarius, I told him he owed them two – then pocketed the extra coin for myself. If he argued about it, I had only to threaten him with arrest by a Roman soldier. A simple ploy that made me rich, but at the same time poor. Still puzzled? Well, I was a rich man – fine house, servants, stylish clothes, rings on my fingers. But, at the same time, I was desperately poor. You see, I had no friends – everyone hated me! I was a cheat, a crook who made money out of his own people while serving an enemy emperor. My only friends were the other tax collectors and they were as bad as me – if not worse. So, why am I telling you all this? Because it's history! It's all over! My life is now rich, and I mean *really* rich! There are things in my life now that are really worth something – not fine houses, or stylish clothes, or even jewellery! No, I mean people. Good people. God's people! People I love, and who love me! And it's all down to Jesus. Yes, Jesus! Jesus, who they call the Son of God. If it wasn't for him, I'd still be a rich man – rich, but miserable – and very lonely. How did it all happen? Well, one day I was in town, and suddenly people were running everywhere.

C 1: It's Jesus!

C 2: Jesus! You know – the miracle-worker, the healer, the one who tells us about God, the one who makes God real!

C 1: He's coming down the street now!

N: Everyone was going mad trying to see him, trying to touch him. Well, I suddenly wanted to see him as well. I'd heard all about him – who hadn't? – but now I wanted to meet him. Me! The biggest sinner in town! I wanted to meet Jesus. So, what did I do? I dashed out into the street and tried to catch a glimpse of him. Easy? Not for me! It's very hard to see in a crowd of people when you're as short as me. And would they let me through? Not likely! Don't forget – they hated me!

C 2: Get out of the way! Clear off! Jesus doesn't want to see the likes of you!

N: But I wanted to see him. So what could I do? Then I spotted it! A tree! Hanging over the road. I ran ahead and started to climb it. Just what I needed: a nice low tree, easy to climb but just tall enough to give a really good view as Jesus passed underneath – and to keep me safe from the crowd if they turned nasty. But I had to be quick! I hadn't climbed a tree since I was a kid. I made it with seconds to spare! And there I was – up in the branches as Jesus came along with his friends. People were trying to touch him as he went past. And then, well, I nearly fell out of the tree! Just as he got under the tree, Jesus stopped and looked up and stared right into my eyes. He seemed to know me!

C 1: Zacchaeus, come down! I want to have dinner with you at your house.

C 2: Me?

N: I couldn't believe it! No one else could, either! Everyone went quiet.

C 1: Him? Doesn't Jesus know who he is? He's a thief!

N: There was a moment's silence. Then I sprang into action! I didn't need to be asked twice! I was down that tree like a shot and off up the road to my house. Well, you've got to get everything just right when you've got an important guest like Jesus! I soon got the servants organised.

C 2: Meat, bread, wine, fruit – bring them! Quickly!

N: There was no shortage of them in my house! And then, there he was – Jesus! Right next to me – smiling, eating, chatting, enjoying himself! In my home! Then, when everyone was full, the room suddenly went quiet. Why? Well, I was standing up. I knew I had something important to say, and everyone was waiting to hear what it was. I suddenly felt nervous, but very, very happy. I cleared my throat. Jesus was looking at me – as if he knew what I was going to say – almost before I did!

C 1: Er, welcome to my house, Master... and... er... thank you for being my guest... and my friend.

N: People were starting to clap – quietly – you know, the polite kind of clapping that means they don't know what's coming next. But I raised my hand and they all stopped. I hadn't finished!

C 2: I know I'm a sinner. A bad one! Most people wouldn't be seen dead with me!

C 1: I'm a thief and a cheat. But now that you've come to my house, Jesus, all that's going to change!

C 2: I'll never cheat or steal again.

C 1: But, what's more, I want a fresh start, so I'm giving half my money to the poor.

C 2: And I'm paying back those I've cheated four times over!

N: Well, by this time I'd said all I wanted – so I sat down. You could have heard a pin drop! Everyone was gobsmacked! Then Jesus spoke and he had the biggest smile on his face.

C 1: Today, in this house, a life has been saved! Zacchaeus has begun to live God's way. And this is exactly why I have come – to search for those who have lost their way and bring them back to God.

Assembly: MY NAME IS ZACCHAEUS

THEME: *For Christians, God's love outweighs everything else*

This play is based on the story of Zacchaeus, which can be found in Luke 19:1–10.

You will need:

a large pair of scales with pans; a weight; about 15 slips of paper; one slip of paper reading 'God's Love'; felt-tip pens

Introduction

In the play, Zacchaeus said that he was poor when he was rich, and when he became poorer he became richer! What did he mean? Ask the pupils what he was rich in at the beginning of the play (money, possessions) and what he was poor in (friends, happiness). What was he poor in at the end of the play? And what was he rich in then? If we say that someone is rich now, what do we usually mean? What would we expect him or her to have? On each piece of paper, write down one of their suggestions. (Depending on the age of the pupils, you can write down categories – such as 'possessions', or actual articles – such as 'a pony'.) When they have named the obvious things, ask them to think more deeply. Zacchaeus said he was poor in friends and in things like love and happiness. What does it mean to be rich in friends or in happiness? Discuss these ideas with them. Write these ideas on additional slips of paper.

Core material

Choose some pupils and ask each to hold up one of the slips, reminding the others what each one says. Point out that there are two groups of possessions here – physical possessions like money and the things that money can buy, and another group of possessions like love and friends that money cannot buy. Ask the pupils to divide themselves into the two groups. Ask the others if they are right. Collect the slips in the two groups, placing one group in each pan on the scales. Explain that we are going to use the weight to show which side we think is 'heavier' or more important. If the importance of the real things was being weighed, which side would Zacchaeus have said would be the heavier or more important? (Answer – the ones he could not buy. Put the weight onto this side and let it sink down.) What do they think? It is very nice to have a lot of money and to be able to buy just what you want, but which group would make you happier? Discuss this with them, asking such questions as 'Which group would last longer?', 'Which group would be more help if you were ill or miserable?' Would they leave the weight where it is or not?

Christians would arrange these possessions differently again. Show them the slip with 'God's Love' written on it. Christians believe that nothing else is as important as knowing that God loves them. Put all the other slips in one pan, and this slip in the other, with the weight. This doesn't mean that if Christians have God's love, they have nothing else! They believe that God will give them all the other possessions they need, but his love is still the most important possession to them.

Prayer/Reflection

Father, help us to weigh the importance of things as we grow up, and to see that some things are more valuable than others and are worth looking for and looking after.

Music suggestions

- Whether you're one, 284, *Junior Praise*; 196, *Children's Praise*
- Father, I know that you are good, 43, *A Year of Celebration*
- God is love, 36, *The Complete Come and Praise*

Background notes

- Tax collectors worked for the Romans and were seen as collaborators. Extortion was easy, with the extra money going straight into their own purses. Zacchaeus was a chief tax collector for the whole district.
- Jewish law demanded that a thief should give back the amount he stole, plus an extra fifth. Zacchaeus gives much more as a sign of his changed life.

Sketch: A GIFT TO WARM THE MASTER'S HEART

CHARACTERS

NARRATOR (N)

CHORUS 1 (C 1)

CHORUS 2 (C 2)

This play is narrated by one of Jesus' disciples. The choruses can mime the actions described by him and by the Narrator.

N: I never liked it – the way people brought money to the temple, as offerings. Rich people! They would march in as if they owned the place, then stop by the money jars and wait – yes – wait until everyone was looking at them! Then they would drop in their coins with a loud…

C 1: CLANG!

N: … as if to say…

C 2: Look how good I am! I've given a big bag of money! Won't God be pleased with me.

N: As if God would be pleased by their little performance! I've always wondered what kind of gift would really please God. Then, one day, we were in the temple courts with Jesus, watching this sickening show of generosity by rich visitors when Jesus tapped me on the shoulder.

C 1: Look!

C 2: What, Master?

C 1: That old woman!

N: Then we saw her – an old woman – very poor, judging by her clothes. Bent nearly double, shuffling in without a sound – almost as if she had no right to be there. Up to the money jars she went and, taking two small coins from her shawl, slipped them in – without a sound! Jesus smiled.

C 2: What, Master?

C 1: Who gave more – the old woman or those rich people?

N: We shrugged our shoulders.

C 2: The rich people, Master – big bags of coins. She only gave two small coins!

N: He smiled again.

C 1: Ah, but she gave all she had – everything!

N: Then I saw it! Jesus was right. He always saw to the heart of the matter. They had given only a tiny part of their wealth. She, though very poor, had given all. I had witnessed an act that warmed the Master's heart. Now I knew what kind of gift would please God! By giving all, the old woman had put her trust totally in God.

Assembly: A GIFT TO WARM THE MASTER'S HEART

THEME: *Real giving*

This play is based on the story of the widow's gift, which can be found in Luke 21:1–4.

You will need:

a selection of gifts you or someone else have been given (or choose some possible examples). Include one or two of obvious value, such as jewellery. Include one which has little obvious value, but which is valuable because of its donor or the cost of it to you in non-financial terms.

Introduction

Explain that you have brought in a selection of gifts, and say that you want the pupils to arrange them in order of value. Show them each one, giving them some idea of its value in terms of what it is made of, where it is from, age, rarity, etc. Which do they think is the most valuable? Continue until they are all in order. Then tell them that, in fact, to you the most valuable is one of the least expensive ones. Explain what makes this object valuable to you. Ask if they have articles that are very valuable to them, even though other people would say that they are worthless – but do not expect them to tell you what they are!

Core material

In the play, Jesus said that the most valuable gift was the widow's. He was not looking at the value of the gifts themselves, but at the reasons why they were given. Ask the pupils why the rich men gave so much. Why did the widow give so little? This was all she had – why did she give so much? Discuss the fact that she was left with no money to live on. She gave all she had because she loved God. She trusted him, too, because she was left with nothing. She believed that he would take care of her. But even if he didn't, she was still going to give him all she had because she loved him.

Ask the pupils to imagine that they have been given a giant bar of chocolate. Would they find it easy to give a few squares to their friends? Why? What if they had just two squares left – would they find it easy to give those to their friends? It is easy to give when we have a lot, but not so easy when we have little ourselves. In the country of Romania, there are many very poor people. One organisation collects food and medicine and toys, and visits Romania to give these to the people who really need them. One day, they had nearly run out of food to give, when an elderly woman came to them. All they could give her was one chocolate bar. She took this and thanked them. Then they watched as she opened the wrapper and carefully broke the bar into ten tiny pieces so that she could give a piece to each member of her family. She had very little, but she gave nearly all of it away because she loved them.

Prayer/Reflection

There are many things we can share in life. Think about this story, and then listen.

Chocolate, sweets and biscuits,
Games and play and toys,
Love and time need sharing, too,
And homes and hopes and cares.

Music suggestions

- Jesus is pleased when I share, 109, *Children's Praise*
- Bread for the world, 75, *The Complete Come and Praise*

Background notes

- The widow actually gave two of the smallest coins, two lepta. Widows with no family to provide for them were often extremely poor.
- This episode took place in the Women's Court of the temple, where there were thirteen large offering boxes for people's contributions to the upkeep of the temple.

Information about Romania by kind permission of Samaritan's Purse International Ltd, Victoria House, Victoria Road, Buckhurst Hill, Essex, IG9 5EX.

NOTES ABOUT PARABLES

Jesus often used stories in his teaching. His stories have a meaning. Stories are a useful tool in teaching for several reasons, including:

- they help people understand and remember things;
- they involve the imagination as well as the intellect;
- sensitive issues – such as discrimination and self-criticism – are easier to comment on in a story;
- interpreting a story for themselves gives listeners an active role;
- use of everyday objects and situations makes the teaching more acceptable and accessible to people;
- in biblical times, the telling of and listening to stories was a familiar situation to many people.

Most of Jesus' stories were of the type called parables. In a parable, things are literally 'put side by side': one person or object is represented by another, to enable the listener to understand concepts more easily and to be open to new interpretations of familiar ideas. So, in the parable of the lost son, the father is like a picture of God. Parables have a meaning which can be difficult to unravel. This is where Jon Webster's retellings are particularly useful. It is important to be aware that these stories are usually not allegories: too close or consistent parallels are not intended, and should not be sought. (But see page 94 about the parable of the sower.)

Sketch: THE TWO SONS

CHARACTERS

NARRATOR (N)

CHORUS (C)

N: There was once an old farmer…

C: Ooo–aaah!

N: … who had two sons. Well, one day he asked his first son to go to the fields for him. But the son just said…

C: Can't be bothered!

N: So the farmer asked his second son to go. And he said…

C: Of course, Dad!

N: But he didn't go.

C: What a nuisance!

N: But later the first son thought…

C: OK, let's go!

N: And he went to the field for his father. Now, it's quiz time! (*In style of a presenter of a TV game show.*) For today's star prize I want you to tell me, which son really helped his father? Was it: (a) the first son who said…

C: Can't be bothered!

N: … but went in the end? Or was it (b) the second son who said…

C: Of course, Dad!

N: … but never went?

C: Er… er… er… Give us a clue!

N: Come on, I must have an answer!

C: It was…

N: Yes?

C: It was…

N: Yes?

C: It was…

N: Yes?

C: … the first son!

N: Congratulations! You have won…

C: (*Musical build-up.*) Da-da-da-da!

N: … a half-day trip to Skegness in January!

C: Y-e-s!

Assembly: THE TWO SONS

THEME: *Words and actions*

This play is based on the parable of the two sons, which can be found in Matthew 21:28–32.

Introduction

(You might like to pause the action of the sketch at the point at which the Narrator poses the question. End with his speech, '... but never went?' Ask the pupils to vote for which of the sons they each think 'really helped his father'. When you have done this, resume the play back at 'Now it's quiz time!' to pick up the action for them.)

This sketch is based on one of the parables Jesus told. A parable is a type of story which has a hidden meaning. Jesus told parables to help the people listening to understand what he was teaching them. We live in a very different world to those people, and sometimes we need a lot of explanation before we can understand the parable. But Christians believe that the teaching of Jesus applies to the world today, just as it applied in the past, because God and people are still the same. This parable's story is quite easy to understand: the first brother refused to obey and help his father, but then changed his mind, and the second brother said he would obey and help, but didn't. But the parable's meaning is not so easy to understand.

Core material

In the parable, Jesus is using the father as a picture of God. God has made laws and has asked people to behave in a certain way, that is to obey those laws. Jesus said that the two brothers were like the people who hear and learn about what God wants them to do.

Some of these people say, 'Not likely! I'm not going to obey God. I've got my own life to lead.' But later, they change their mind. They decide that God only wants to help them, and that they can't be happy unless they do obey him. Ask the pupils which brother these people are like. Jesus said that some people he knew were like this. They had started off not wanting to obey God, but they had changed their minds later on, and were now obeying him.

Jesus also said that other people – especially some of the religious leaders who should have been showing the others how to obey God – were like the second son. They had promised to obey God, but then decided it was too much bother, and they had stopped obeying him.

Tell the pupils you've got another question for them, but without a prize this time! Is Jesus saying that words or actions are more important? It's no good saying you'll do something, and then not doing it! Promises are no good unless you keep them.

Reflection

Here's another quiz, but one you need only answer to yourself.

When you say you'll help someone, do you:

a) say it to stop them nagging you?

b) say it to make them think you are a good person?

c) say it because you feel you should offer to do something?

d) say it because you really are going to help them?

Think about it!

Music suggestions

- In our work and in our play, 108, *Junior Praise*
- Break out, 91, *The Complete Come and Praise*

Background notes

- The father was not asking for anything excessive when he asked his sons to work. Sons would work on the family farm, which was probably just a small plot of land.

The following plays (and some in the puppet play section) deal with some of the parables told by Jesus. All, to a greater or lesser extent, remove them from their contemporary setting and retell them in a modern context. The Bible references to the original parables are given for those who wish to use these as well, perhaps as introductions to the plays.

Sketch: THE UNFORGIVING ROUNDERS PLAYER

CHARACTERS
NARRATOR (N)
CHORUS (C)

N: There was once a school rounders team that won all the local cups.

C: Hooray! (*All wave.*)

N: But in this team there was one star player.

C: What a star!

N: She was great at catching...

C: (*All mime catching.*)

N: excellent at bowling...

C: (*All mime bowling.*)

N: brilliant at batting...

C: (*All mime batting.*)

N: and the fastest runner in the school.

C: Whoosh! (*All look from right to left very, very quickly.*)

N: As I said, she was the star of the team.

C: Hooray!

N: But the team was never the same if she didn't play.

C: Eh? (*All scratch heads.*)

N: Well, what I mean is, although the others were pretty good players...

C: Yes?

N: Well, if Sally wasn't playing, the team didn't win!

C: Oh!

N: One day the team had a really important game. They were in the final of the District Cup. But where was Sally?

C: (*All look round and keep looking at watches, very worried.*)

N: The time for the game arrived, but Sally just didn't turn up.

C: Oh, no! (*All throw up hands in dismay.*)

N: Sure enough, the team lost the game. They all did their best, but they missed Sally's catching...

C: (*All mime catching.*)

N: bowling...

C: (*All mime bowling.*)

N: batting...

C: (*All mime batting.*)

N: and running.

C: Whoosh! (*Mime looking from right to left very quickly.*)

N: Mr Green, the teacher, was not very pleased when he got back to school and found Sally playing on her bike outside the gate.

C: (*All tut-tut-tut and shake heads.*)

N: Mr Green told Sally she had let the side down. He was really disappointed in her.

C: (*All wag fingers.*)

N: He was going to tell her parents, he said.

C: Oh, no!

N: Sally knew her parents would ground her because they thought she had been playing rounders for the school. So she said…

C: Sorry!

N: Sally was very relieved when Mr Green let her off.

C: Thanks! (*Wipe foreheads.*)

N: But then she blew it all! She was just on her way home when she bumped into Jenny. Jenny owed Sally some sweets and Sally wanted them right now.

C: Please let me off!

N: But Sally grabbed Jenny's sweets.

C: (*Grab and mime eating delicious sweets.*) M-m-m! Nice!

N: Jenny began to cry.

C: Boo-hoo! (*Mime.*)

N: Mr Green asked her what was the matter. When she told him, he was furious and went straight round to Sally's house. Sally's mum and dad were not very happy.

C: You're grounded!

N: Sally was really sorry now. But she had to learn the hard way that if someone lets you off something really big, you have to be just as forgiving and let others off as well – even really small things, like…

C: … sweets!

Assembly: THE UNFORGIVING ROUNDERS PLAYER

THEME: *Treating others as we treat ourselves*

This is based on the parable of the unforgiving servant in Matthew 18:23–35.

Introduction

This play is about forgiveness. Ensure the pupils know what this means. The play is about being forgiven when we say sorry, and about forgiving others when they say sorry. Sally expected to be forgiven, but she didn't want to forgive Jenny. What Sally had done was far worse than what Jenny had done. Sally had let the whole team down and had lied to her parents. Jenny just owed Sally a few sweets. Read to the pupils the parable on which this play is based. Help them to link the 'pairs' in the two stories, eg Sally is the first servant who owed a lot of money. But who was Jesus thinking of when he wrote this parable?

Core material

Explain or recap on the way in which characters in parables are pictures of – or stand for – someone else (see page 33). The king is a picture of God. The money which is owed is a picture of all the wrong things the people have done. So the first servant has done many things which have upset God. God forgives this first man when he says sorry, but then the man refuses to forgive another man who owes him just a little money. This means that this man has only done a few things wrong. Jesus is saying that the first man should forgive the other, just as he was forgiven himself.

Jesus taught his followers a prayer which has become famous. It is called the Lord's Prayer. One part of it says, 'Forgive us, God, for doing wrong things, just as we forgive other people who have done wrong things to us.' Jesus was saying that we cannot ask for forgiveness if we do not forgive other people. Sally and the first servant had two different rules about forgiveness: one for themselves which said, 'I should be forgiven!' and one for other people that said, 'They should not be forgiven!' Jesus said a strange thing about people like this. He said, 'Do not complain about the speck of sawdust in someone else's eye while you are ignoring the plank of wood in your own eye! How can you see clearly to take out that speck of sawdust when you have a plank in your own eye?' (Matthew 7:3,4 paraphrased) Now, you can have a speck of sawdust in your eye, but you can't walk around with a plank in it! Jesus meant this to be a picture of something else. Ask if anyone can explain it, and if not say: he meant that some people complain about other people's small faults, but they ignore their own faults, even when these are much larger. We need to have the same set of rules for ourselves and for other people. We should not expect others to behave better than we do. If they make mistakes, we need to admit that we make mistakes too – and sometimes our mistakes are even worse than theirs!

Prayer/Reflection

It is very easy to spot other people's mistakes in life.

It is not so easy to admit we make mistakes too.

Help us to see ourselves as we really are, not as we would like others to see us.

Help us to admit when we are wrong, and help us not to make the same mistakes again.

Music suggestions

- Make me a channel of your peace, 161, *Junior Praise*
- Put your hand in the hand, 206, *Junior Praise*

Sketch: THE RICH TENNIS STAR

CHARACTERS
NARRATOR (N)
CHORUS (C)

N: A few years ago near here, a young girl was watching Wimbledon on TV.

C: (*Mime serving with a big grunt.*)

N: She liked to play tennis in the garden.

C: (*Mime playing.*)

N: She was a real smash, in more ways than one! (*Smashing sound.*)

C: Clear off!

N: She decided she wanted to play at Wimbledon one day. She wanted to be…

C: … rich and famous!

N: But that meant lots of hard practice.

C: (*Mime.*)

N: Whenever her little brother wanted a game, she just said…

C: … too busy! (*Mime practising.*)

N: But all that practice began to pay off. At school she won the Carruthers-Brown Trophy for Lawn Tennis.

C: Three cheers for Fiona: hip, hip, hooray! (*All clap.*)

N: Then it was back to the hard practice.

C: (*Mime.*)

N: She rose to the top very quickly.

C: (*Mime newspaper sellers.*) Extra! Extra! Read all about it! Local tennis star picked for England!

N: In her first Wimbledon, she got through to the final.

C: (*Mime looking from side to side as they watch the game.*)

N: She played brilliantly!

C: Match point!

N: It was nerve-racking!

C: Quiet please! (*Mime serving with a grunt.*)

N: She served an ace!

C: Game, set and match! (*Clap and cheer.*)

N: All that practice paid off – she had a tennis racket named after her.

C: Buy my racket!

N: And her own brand of tennis shoes.

C: Buy my shoes!

N: She had…

C: … loads of dosh!

N: She was a megastar. But it didn't seem to make her happy. She never seemed to be satisfied.

C: (*Mime practising.*)

C: Autograph, please, Fiona!

N: She didn't care about others – only herself and staying at the top.

C: Too busy! (*Mime practising.*)

N: The vicar asked her to do some coaching with the children at a school nearby.

C: Too busy! (*Mime practising.*)

N: She didn't care about other people and she didn't care about God. She just wanted to practise for the French Open.

C: (*Mime.*)

N: Then she had a brilliant idea. She

bought a…

C: … big house… (*Arms wide open.*)

N: … with its own tennis court, and lots of…

C: … barbed wire… (*Mime practising.*)

N: … to keep the fans out!

C: Great! (*Mime.*)

N: That night, the cleaning lady switched on the video of her Wimbledon triumph so that Fiona could watch it again, and said…

C: Ta-ra!

N: But Fiona was too busy watching.

C: Huh! (*Fold arms.*)

N: One day she'd have time to sign autographs and coach children.

C: Really?

N: One day, she'd even have time to think about God, as the vicar wanted her to.

C: Really?

N: But right now she was…

C: … too busy!

N: But, although she didn't know it, her time had run out.

C: Uuuugh! (*Clutch chests.*)

N: All that hard work had caught up with her.

C: Extra! Extra! Read all about it! Tennis star dead!

N: The papers reported a quiet funeral. Well, to be honest, no one came! Guess why?

Assembly: THE RICH TENNIS STAR

THEME: Priorities

This play is based on the parable of the rich fool, which can be found in Luke 12:13–21.

Introduction

Ask the pupils to tell you what things are important in their lives. You could start them off by giving an example of your own – for instance, your job or your hobby. Take a few examples, and then ask them to think about these things, and to decide what is the most important thing in their own lives. Tell them that they don't have to tell anyone else what this is. In the play, what was the most important thing in Fiona's life? This play is based on a parable Jesus told about a man who was only interested in his wealth. The most important thing in his life was money!

Core material

Ask the pupils: is there anything wrong with having money or in being good at something like tennis? In our society, we all need money, and many people enjoy playing different sports, and watching those who are very good at them. The play and the parable are not saying that these things are wrong. What they are saying is that it is wrong when something like money or sport takes over a person's whole life – as they did in the two stories. It is a question of priorities. A person's priorities are the things that matter to them, in the order of their importance to them. How many pupils at the beginning decided that watching television was important to them? There is nothing wrong with watching some television. But if a person wants to do nothing else but watch television, then that is not a helpful or healthy way to live. Most people enjoy their food, but few would say that it is the most important thing in their lives. It is all a question of deciding what really matters, and getting everything balanced in your life. It is easy to become obsessed with something, so that it is the only thing you can think of all day. Some people are like this with new computer games, or with the 'soaps' on television. This means they miss many other things that they would enjoy doing or seeing because they are too busy to spare the time.

Christians believe that liking something too much in this way means that they are not following God as he wants them to. They believe that the most important thing to them should be finding out what God wants them to do, and then doing it. Jesus said, 'You should make pleasing God and living as his friend the most important thing in your lives.'

Everybody needs a balance of things in their lives. Have they heard the old saying: 'All work and no play makes Jack a dull boy'? (Explain that dull means tired, bored and boring here.) This works the other way too. Can they think of suitable endings for the following:

'All play and no work makes Jill...'
'All television and no sport makes Fred...'
'All sport and no television makes Louise...'

Can they think of another sentence – but not about a real person?

Reflection

Ask the pupils to sit quietly while you read this to them.

Think about your life and about how you spend your time. As you grow up, there will be more and more activities you want to be involved in. There will be more and more work to do, too. Will it be easy to balance all these? How will you do it?

Prayer

Father, help us to decide which things really matter to us. Help us not to spend too much time and effort on something that does not help us, and which makes life more difficult for our friends and families.

Music suggestions

- Light up the fire, 28, *Junior Praise*; 55, *The Complete Come and Praise*
- Your ways are higher than mine, 295, *Junior Praise*

Background notes

- 'Fool' in the Bible is not used as we would use it, in almost a comical sense. A fool was far worse than just a silly or thoughtless person.
- The Jewish Scriptures taught that wealth was to be shared with the poor, not just hoarded.

Sketch: THE WEDDING FEAST

CHARACTERS
NARRATOR (N)
CHORUS (ALL)

N: There was once a rich lady called Lady Bountiful whose son…

ALL: (*In a posh voice.*)… Cecil…

N: … was engaged to marry…

ALL: (*In a posh voice.*)… Rowena!

N: They were made for each other!

ALL: (*In a posh voice.*) Such a charming girl!

N: Lady Bountiful was determined to throw a splendid party for the wedding. She hired Nottingham Castle for the reception. All the guests would eat the very best food…

ALL: … smoked salmon!

N: For the disco, she booked none other than…

ALL: … the Flying Hamsters! (*All scream.*)

N: Now, Lady Bountiful sat down to write her invitations. She asked all the richest and most important people in the land, such as…

ALL: (*Like a butler announcing guests.*) … the Duke of Mudford!

N: But he said he could not come.

ALL: (*Deep, posh voice.*) Sorry, my horse is in the Derby that day.

N: Lady Bountiful was very disappointed. She wrote to Lady Ponsonby-Smythe.

ALL: (*In a very posh voice.*) I was at school with a real-life Princess – jolly hockey sticks!

N: But she couldn't come either.

ALL: Sorry! I'm off skiing at Klosters!

N: Lady Bountiful was very disappointed. She asked the Archbishop of Barnsley.

ALL: (*Intoned.*) Sorry! I have to write my sermon.

N: Lady Bountiful was in tears.

ALL: Oh dear! (*All cry.*)

N: She was so disappointed.

ALL: Oh dear! (*All cry.*)

N: What a disaster!

ALL: OH DEAR! (*All cry.*) They'll never know what they've missed!

N: She decided to invite ordinary people like…

ALL: … you and me! (*Point into audience and at themselves.*)

N: She invited the lady from the chippy. She came along.

ALL: This beats jumbo sausages any day!

N: She invited her local police officer.

ALL: 'Ello, 'ello, 'ello. (*Knee-bending routine.*) Better than the police station canteen.

N: She invited the rag and bone man. He came too.

ALL: Lovely Rosey Lee – that's a cup o' tea!

N: She invited a football supporter, too.

ALL: Here we go, here we go, here we go! (*Hold up arms and sway.*)

N: Lady Bountiful was delighted.

ALL: Smashing!

N: The ordinary people had a great time.

ALL: What a party!

N: So did Cecil and Rowena.

ALL: Happy honeymoon!

Assembly: THE WEDDING FEAST

THEME: *God's invitation*

This is based on the parable of the great banquet found in Luke 14:15–24.

You will need:

large sheet of paper plus smaller ones; felt-tip pens; invitations prepared in advance (optional)

Introduction

How many of the pupils still hold or have held birthday parties? Ask them to think about their dream birthday party, if they could choose any activity and any location. Ask for a few examples. Combine two or three of the suggestions into an invitation to a 'Mega Birthday Party', and write it on the sheet of paper, beginning 'You are invited to…' Ask them to imagine that everything has been booked and arranged, and it is now time to invite their friends and tell them all about it. Choose a pupil to be the host/ess, and tell her to invite other pupils chosen by you. They are all to refuse, making up excuses if they wish. Ask the host/ess how (s)he would feel if this really happened. That is what happened to the woman in the play. What did she decide to do instead? Would the pupils do the same, rather than lose the party altogether?

Core material

This play is very similar to Jesus' parable on which it is based. Read or tell them the original. Jesus was saying that living as God's friend was like going to the greatest feast or party ever held. God was like the man who was holding this feast. He had sent out many invitations – but all the people who had received them said they could not go. They all had good excuses for saying no, but God was still upset. He wanted people to be his friends, so he invited other people. Jesus meant that some people had been invited to be God's friends. Write 'You are invited to become God's friend' on one of the smaller sheets of paper. But everyone refused. It was as if they had torn up the invitation. (do so) They had let other things become more important than friendship with God. So God asked other people (write out another invitation), and they were happy to become God's friends – just as the second group of people enjoyed the feast.

When we go to other people's houses, we like to feel that they really want us there and are pleased to see us. We like to feel relaxed and 'at home' when we visit people. Ask the pupils what makes them feel like this when they go to other people's houses. The way they are greeted and the food they are offered will probably be mentioned, but if not, raise these issues yourself. There is a verse in the Bible which says: 'God welcomes me to his banqueting table, and his banner over me is love.' Imagine a table spread with all the foods and drinks all of you most like to eat, and a notice saying: 'Eat as much as you like!' That is a banquet! The verse says that God welcomes his friends. When he says, 'It's nice to see you,' he really means it! People often have banners now at parties: ask the pupils what these might say. The banner in the verse is like a picture of the way God surrounds his friends with love. It is as if he has a banner over every friend's head saying, 'I love this person!' Christians believe that accepting and saying 'Yes' to God's invitation to be his friend is like joining the greatest and happiest party ever. But this party, they believe, will never end.

Prayer/Reflection

Thank you, Father, that your invitation is an open invitation: it has everyone's name on it. You want everyone to be your friend and to come to your party.

Music suggestions

- He brought me to his banqueting house, 73, *Junior Praise*
- The wedding banquet, 157, *A Year of Celebration*

Background notes

- In the parable, the invited people all give reasonable excuses: being newly-married or having to plough land were reasons for being excused military service. But these people have not realised this invitation is far more important than being called-up to fight!

Sketch: OPEN ALL HOURS

CHARACTERS

NARRATOR (N)

CHORUS (C)

N: There was once an old newsagent who ran a corner shop.

C: (*With a Northern accent.*) Open all hours!

N: One day, Albert – that was his name – had a new paper boy.

C: Wayne's the name. (*All wave.*)

N: Wayne was really keen to get started.

C: I'm saving for a new mountain bike.

N: Albert tried to give him instructions for his paper round.

C: (*All pupils, individually, mutter directions such as 'go right, then left, then second right, then…', pointing with arms.*)

N: But Wayne was too excited to listen.

C: See ya! Back soon! (*Wave.*)

N: The old newsagent tried to warn him.

C: Hang about! (*Beckon with arms.*)

N: But it was too late.

C: (*Fold arms, shake heads.*)

N: Wayne was gone… then the fog came down. Old Mrs Jones came in for a Radio Times.

C: (*Croaky voice.*) I'm stopping in tonight.

N: The fog got thicker. But where was Wayne? Police Officer Plod came in for some throat sweets.

C: 'Ello, 'ello, 'ello! (*Knee-bending, hands behind back act.*) It's so thick I can hardly see past my nose.

N: And the fog got thicker. But where was Wayne? Mavis came in for some crisps.

C: They've stopped the buses. The drivers can't see!

N: And the fog got thicker still. But where was Wayne? At last, the old newsagent put on his cap…

C: (*Mime.*)

N: … and his scarf.

C: (*Mime.*)

N: His wife didn't want him to go.

C: Think of your chest!

N: It was true. The doctor had said…

C: It could kill you! (*Wag finger.*)

N: But he wouldn't listen to his wife. All he knew was that Wayne was…

C: … lost! (*Plaintive cry.*)

N: He went out into the foggy streets, calling…

C: (*Hands cupped to mouth.*) Wayne! Wayne!

N: No reply. He tried again…

C: Wayne! Wayne!

N: Still no reply.

C: Wayne! Wayne! (*Starts coughing.*)

N: Then he heard a small voice, seemingly miles away.

C: Help! Mr Higginbotham, I'm lost!

N: Albert struggled through the fog, his lungs aching.

C: Come on, Wayne, I think we deserve a nice cup of tea.

N: And so they delivered the rest of the papers together, and got safely home.

C: (*Mime pushing papers through letter boxes.*) We'll make a paper boy of you yet!

Assembly: OPEN ALL HOURS

THEME: *God cares for everybody*

This play is based on the parable of the lost sheep, which can be found in Luke 15:1–7. It also uses Jesus' description of himself as the good Shepherd in John 10:14.

Bible verses

'Sparrows are worth very little to people – but God knows what is happening to each one of them... and you are worth far more than they are!' Luke 12:6,7 *(paraphrase)*

You will need:

pencil and paper (to record votes)

Introduction

Ask the pupils who they think is the most important person in the country. Choose two or three of their suggestions, and ask them to give you their reasons for suggesting these people. Then ask them all to vote for one of the suggested people. Who won? What made that person 'important'? Is that person really different from us? Are they really worth more than we are? Or is it just their power or their position or their wealth that makes them important?

Christians believe that we are all important to God. He doesn't think one person is more important than other people. The play is based on one of Jesus' parables about a lost sheep. Jesus used this parable to show the people that everyone is important to God.

Core material

There was once a shepherd who had a hundred sheep. He knew all of them, and liked every one of them. Every day, he led them to good grass and fresh water. He made sure that they had shade to rest in when the sun was too hot. He kept them safe from wild animals, and rescued them from rocky cliffs and sharp thorns. At night, he counted them carefully into the shelter he had built for them. He piled up rocks across its door, and then lay down, wrapped in his cloak, across the door, so that his sheep were safe from robbers and wild animals. But even though he took such good care of them, the sheep still behaved like sheep. They were still silly and easily frightened. They still went where he told them not to go. They still thought that they knew best!

One night, as he counted the sheep, he realised that one was missing. He hurried over the hill, to the camp where his friend was looking after his own sheep. 'Could you make sure my sheep are safe until I come back?' he asked.

His friend laughed. 'You're surely not setting off again at this time of the night to find just one stupid sheep, are you?' he asked. 'You've still got ninety-nine sheep. Forget about the other one!'

But the shepherd shook his head. 'I have to find her and look after her. She needs me. She's important!' he said, and he set off. It was a dark, cold night, and he searched for a long time. But at last he heard the bleating of the frightened sheep. She was caught in a thorn bush. Gently, he untangled her wool and carried her home. 'Look!' he told his friend. 'I've found her! She's safe! Tomorrow I will have a party to celebrate – and you're invited!'

Christians believe that God is like that 'good shepherd'. No matter how many people are his friends, he is still really pleased when someone new becomes his friend, because he loves everyone. Everyone is important to him. And Christians believe that Jesus is like that shepherd too, because he died so that everyone could become friends with God.

Prayer/Reflection

Thank you, Father, that you love all of us the same. Thank you that Jesus showed us that love in action.

OR

Do you value everyone? Do you think that everyone is worth the same? Think about it – is there anyone you treat differently because you think they are not as good as you? Is this fair?

Music suggestions

- One and two, 445, *Junior Praise 2*; 134, *Children's Praise*
- God is love, 36, *The Complete Come and Praise*
- The Lord, the Lord, 108, *The Complete Come and Praise*

Background notes

- Shepherds had to defend themselves and their sheep from wild animals in dangerous terrain. One weapon was the sling (see page 18). The sheep would be kept in a stone fold at night. Often the shepherd would lie across its gate to protect them.

Sketch: THE SATURDAY NIGHT GOOD SAMARITAN

CHARACTERS

NARRATOR (N)
ALL
CHORUS 1 (C 1)
CHORUS 2 (C 2)

N: Old Mrs Brown was just coming home from…

ALL: … bingo…

N: … in the village hall, when, suddenly, she heard a horrible noise.

ALL: 'Ere we go, 'ere we go, 'ere we go! (*Repeat as football supporters' chant.*)

N: Oh no! It was Billy, the local football hooligan!

ALL: We hate Mudford United! (*Or name of local rival.*)

N: Billy was fed up because his team had lost…

ALL: … ten-nil!

N: He was shouting…

ALL: What a load of rubbish!

N: When he saw old Mrs Brown, he thought…

ALL: (*All click fingers.*)

N: I bet she's got…

ALL: … loads of dosh!

N: He said, Give us a…

ALL: … quid!

N: I want some…

ALL: … chips! M-m-m-m! (*All rub tummies.*)

N: But she said…

ALL: No!

N: Billy was disappointed.

ALL: Aaah!

N: So he snatched her handbag…

ALL: Grab! (*Mime.*)

N: … and went off singing…

ALL: Walk on, walk on, with hope in your heart… (*etc*)

N: Mrs Brown was scared on her own in the dark, and now she had no bus fare left to get home. She was stuck.

ALL: Help!

N: Then she saw Police Officer Plod.

ALL: 'Ello, 'ello, 'ello! (*Knees bent, arms behind back.*)

N: She asked him to help her, but he said he was…

ALL: … off duty! (*Shake heads.*)

N: Then he went back to the police station to watch…

ALL: … Match of the Day.

N: Mrs Brown was very scared on her own in the dark.

ALL: Help! Help!

N: Then along came Dr Cure-all. Old Mrs Brown asked her for a lift home. But the doctor was on the way to the local hospital to perform a very important operation on (*well-known local character*).

ALL: Next please! (*Mime ringing a desk bell.*)

N: Mrs Brown was very, very scared on her own in the dark with no bus fare.

ALL: Help! Help! Help!

N: Then along came Lady Fotheringay-Benting – a posh lady who did the flower-arranging at the church. Mrs Brown asked for a lift home in her Rolls Royce. But Lady Fotheringay-Benting was tired.

ALL: (*Yawn.*)

N: She had been busy all day running a…

ALL: … jumble sale…

N: … for…

ALL: … homeless pussy cats. Aaaah!

N: She was going home for a…

ALL: … nice cup of Earl Grey tea!

N: Mrs Brown was very, very, very scared on her own in the dark with no bus fare.

ALL: Help! Help! Help! Help!

N: Then along came Jack-the-Lad, the local hard case.

C 1: Don't hurt me!

C 2: I've got no money!

C 1: I was…

C 2: … mugged!

N: Jack gave her the…

ALL: … bus fare…

N: … and ten pounds for a new…

ALL: … handbag!

N: Then he helped her onto the bus.

ALL: Ding! Ding!

N: All Mrs Brown could say was…

ALL: … Ta very much! Fancy that!

N: Now, let's see who has been listening. Who was the real friend to Mrs Brown? Was it the police officer?

ALL: No!

N: Was it the doctor?

ALL: No!

N: Was it the posh lady from church?

ALL: No!

N: Who was it, then?

ALL: Jack-the-Lad!

N: That's right!

Note: the police officer and the doctor could, of course, be either sex.

Assembly: THE SATURDAY NIGHT GOOD SAMARITAN

THEME: *Who is our neighbour?*

This is based on the parable of the good Samaritan which can be found in Luke 10:25–37.

You will need:

a large sheet of paper with a series of four concentric circles drawn on it. Then, draw a sector (a 'slice of pie') of about an eighth of the circle (a 45° angle at the centre), cutting through the inner circles, and leave this blank when you write in the pupils' suggestions; felt-tip pens

Introduction

Ask the pupils how many people they know. Take a few of their guesses. Show them the sheet of paper, and explain that they are going to think about all the people in the world, and divide them into various categories. Draw a brightly coloured spot in the very centre of the circles, and say that this represents the pupils. So the people in the first, innermost circle will be the people they know best – their 'family'. Write this in the innermost circle. So who do they think will be in the next circle? Label this one 'friends'. These are the two groups of people who are closest to the pupils. The next circle is the people we meet sometimes, without really being friends – for instance, the shopkeeper and the woman in the house on the corner. Label this circle 'People we meet', and write in other suggestions from them. Can any of them guess what the last circle will be? This is for all the people we haven't met. Label it 'People we don't meet', and fill in their suggestions, such as 'the people of Canada', 'the people on Coronation Street'. If neighbours have not been mentioned, ask where they would put them. Show them the sheet, and point out that we have a blank section which cuts through all of the groups of people – their family, friends and both the people they meet and those they don't meet. We'll find out who should be in here.

Core material

The play we have watched is based on the parable of the good Samaritan. Jesus told this parable because someone asked him what he should do to please God. Jesus told him, 'Love God… and love your neighbour as you love yourself.' Now the man already knew this. He realised that he looked silly for asking such an easy question, so he asked another one: 'But who is my neighbour?' Then Jesus told him this story:

> 'A Jewish man was once making a long and dangerous journey when he was attacked by robbers. They stole all he had and left him to die in the hot sun. A priest came along – but he hurried on. Then another man, a Levite who helped the priests in the Temple, came by – but he too hurried past. Perhaps they were both frightened that the robbers might still be there, and if they stopped to help, they would not be able to do their jobs at the temple that day. Then a third man came, but he was from Samaria, and the Samaritans were the enemies of the Jews. Surely he wouldn't stop? But he did! He helped the injured man to a house where he could be looked after.'

'So,' said Jesus, 'who was the neighbour to that man?' The man had to admit that the Samaritan, the enemy of his people, had acted as a neighbour.

In the play, Mrs Brown is helped by someone she was afraid of – just as the Jewish man would have been afraid of the Samaritan. Jesus was saying that a neighbour is anyone who needs our help, or anyone who helps us when we need help. So that is who belongs in the blank section, for someone who needs help can be in our family, a friend, someone we talk to, or even someone we have never met and are not likely to meet. Also, anyone in any of these groups might help us if we need help. Write in the blank segment 'Neighbours – people who need our help or who help us'.

Prayer/Reflection

Help us, Father, to recognise people who need our help, even if they are people we do not like or who do not belong to our own little group.

Music suggestions

- Would you walk by, 498, *Junior Praise 2*; 96, *A Year of Celebration*
- When I needed a neighbour, 275, *Junior Praise*; 65, *The Complete Come and Praise*

Background notes

- Jews and Samaritans were long-standing enemies. Jews believed the Samaritans were impure in race and worship. The Jews would take long detours to avoid Samaria. Jesus probably shocked people by going through this region.
- The road was the Wadi Qelt, a very steep and lonely route, and a frequent haunt of robbers. Travellers did their best to avoid travelling it alone.
- The priest and the Levite acted as most prudent people would in the circumstances. They probably suspected this was an ambush set up by the robbers. It was not a safe place in which to offer help. Also, if they had stopped to help, and discovered the man was dead, they would have been barred, according to the Mosaic Law, from their usual temple duties until they had undertaken long and elaborate ceremonial cleansing rituals. The Samaritan behaves in a very brave and self-sacrificing way.
- Priests were responsible for the ritual of the temple – the services of prayer and worship, the sacrifices, and the teaching and interpretation of the Law. Levites acted as assistants to the priests, and were responsible for all the music of the temple, both choral and instrumental.

Sketch: THE LOST CHORD

CHARACTERS

NARRATOR (N)

CHORUS (C)

N: There was once an old musician called Mrs Jones. Not only did she play, she also taught students at a music school not far from here. A conservatoire!

C: Eh?

N: A conservatoire – a music school!

C: Oooooooh!

N: The old lady was very proud of her students and tried to teach them all she knew about music. Some were very talented…

C: (*Clap.*) Beautiful! Magnifico!

N: … while others didn't have such a good ear for music! (*Someone playing 'chopsticks 'on the piano.*)

N: But she taught them as much as she could. When they all left music school, she hoped they would go on playing.

C: I just *love* music! Cool!

N: Alan, one of the class, was playing at the Albert Hall.

C: (*Cough.*) Ssssh! (*Play recording of beautiful music, while we see Alan playing.*) Bravissimo! (*Clap.*)

N: Mrs Jones was proud of Alan and glad he was still playing.

N: Then she visited a recording studio where Kelly was recording her latest album.

C: (*Hands on ears, faces screwed up, singing along to pop music.*)

N: Kelly was soon…

C: … Top of the Pops.

N: Mrs Jones was deafened, but glad that Kelly was still using her music skills. In the High Street, she met Dave. He was busking.

C: (*All sing well-known song, and mime playing instruments.*) Spare a penny, Miss!

N: Mrs Jones was pleased to oblige.

C: Cheers, Mrs Jones!

N: Mrs Jones knew they couldn't all be megastars like Alan or Kelly, but she was glad they were still making music.

C: Sounds great!

N: Then she bumped into Sarah, sitting on the wall with her ghetto blaster. (*Sarah is playing very loud music on the tape recorder.*)

C: Cool!

N: No! Mrs Jones was not a happy lady!

C: Oh!

N: She asked Jane why she wasn't playing music herself. Jane said her own music sounded awful.

C: Way out, man!

N: But Mrs Jones was not amused! She was very disappointed.

C: What a waste! (*She switches off the ghetto blaster and walks off-stage.*)

Assembly: THE LOST CHORD

THEME: *Our talents*

This play is based on the parable of the talents, which can be found in Matthew 25:14–30.

You will need:

20 play or chocolate coins – silver coloured if possible (if you have fewer coins, adjust text below as necessary); large sheet of paper and felt-tip pens for the pupils to use

---

Introduction

The people in the play all shared a talent – for making music. What does the word 'talent' mean? Different people have different talents. Ask the pupils to think about one of their friends in school, who is not to be named, or one of the adults in school. What talent does that person have? Ask for volunteers to write the talent on the sheet or to tell you what to write: several can do this at a time. Wait until you have about twenty suggestions written down. Go through them briefly, and comment how different they are. Say that, if you had all had enough time, you would have been able to write down a talent for everyone in the school, because everyone is talented in at least one thing. Then say that you are special because you have twenty talents! Do they believe you? Produce the coins and count them, saying, 'There you are, twenty talents!' Explain that, in Jesus' time, there was an amount of money called a talent. It had nothing to do with the talents we mean today, but in this parable, one kind of talent stands for the other. The play was about the talents which are skills. The parable it is based on was about the talents meaning money. Both of the stories have the same meaning.

Core material

In the play, Mrs Jones was pleased to see that some of her students were using their skill-talent, and she was disappointed when one of them was not. In the parable Jesus told, a man gave some money-talents to three of his servants, asking them to make use of them. Two did this, investing the money and making more, but the other made no use of the money and hid it, because he was frightened of losing it altogether. When people think about this story, they see the money-talents as a picture of skill-talents. The man who gave the money is like God, who Christians believe gives everyone different skill-talents. Christians believe that these skills are given to people to be used, not to be hidden away. When people use their skills, it brings happiness to themselves and help and happiness to other people.

As you grow up, you will find more and more things at which you are good. It is exciting to explore all of these, and to find out which you enjoy most and what you can do with these skills. Sometimes we don't find out what we can do until we are quite old! It is even more exciting then to discover a talent inside ourselves and to learn how to use it. Sarah was afraid to use her talent because she thought she was not good enough. But if she had carried on trying, she would have improved. In any case, we often think we are not good enough when really we are. We only find out by trying!

Reflection

So many people in our world,

So many different talents!

So many different things each of us can do,

So many different talents!

Do you know yet which talents you have?

Music suggestions

- One day I might, 137, *Children's Praise*
- The wise may bring, 253, *Junior Praise*; 64, *The Complete Come and Praise*

Background notes

- It is believed the talent in the parable was not an actual coin but an amount of money – about 6,000 denarii.

Sketch: A DONKEY FOR A KING

CHARACTERS

PETER

CHORUS 1 (C 1)

CHORUS 2 (C 2)

PETER: I couldn't believe what he was asking us to do!

C 1: Go into the next village. You'll find a donkey tied up with her colt. Bring them to me.

C 2: And if anyone asks what you're doing, Say, 'The Master needs them'.

PETER: We'd followed him for three long years –
Given up our fishing nets,
Left our families,
Traipsed the length of the country –
Footsore we were –
Listened as he spoke,
Watched as he healed the sick,
Shared his trials and tribulations –
The dangers and the hardships.
Now we knew for certain that he was someone different –
No ordinary man!
But now what was he saying to us?
Jesus was like a king to us!
And he was asking us to bring him a donkey!
Surely a king would ride into Jerusalem on a charger?
Now was his moment of triumph!
Everyone would recognise him for who he was,
Just as we had done!
King Jesus!
But not if he rode on a donkey!
But that was his decision,
And no one argued with him.

For a saddle, he was content with a cloak slung over the little creature.
We hoisted him up
And the gentle little beast trotted off
With me leading it by its halter.
And there they were!
The pilgrims!
Some were Galileans like us!
Country folk up for the Passover Feast.
Cheering their hero – Jesus!

C 1: Long live the King!

C 2: God bless the King of Israel!

PETER: They waved palm branches
And threw them on the dusty road.

C 1: Long live the King!

C 2: God bless the King of Israel!

PETER: Men, women and children,
All shouting and singing.
Some threw their cloaks on the road
For the donkey to walk on.

C 1: Long live the King!

C 2: God bless the King of Israel!

PETER: Strangers stopped and asked...

C 1: Who is he?

PETER: And we replied...

C 2: It's Jesus from Nazareth in Galilee!

PETER: It was a heady moment.
Who would have thought that,
Five days later,
His friends would all be missing
When he needed them most?
And that even I, so close to him,
Would say,

ALL: I do not know the man!

Assembly: A DONKEY FOR A KING

THEME: *The Kingship of Jesus*

This story can be found in Matthew 21:1–11.

You will need:

collection of dressing up clothes if possible, including some suitable for a monarch; if not, a roll of wallpaper and felt-tip pens

---

Introduction

Ask if any of the pupils have ever seen a member of the royal family. If so, how were they dressed? Talk about the difference in the clothes worn for formal, state occasions and 'ordinary' events. Choose some pupils to dress another pupil as a king or queen for a formal event such as the State Opening of Parliament. Let them choose suitable clothes from the collection, commenting on their choice as they work. If no clothes are available, draw around a teacher on the wallpaper, and then ask pupils to draw and colour state clothes on the outline. When this is finished, ask them what other things they would expect to see and hear on a televised state occasion or on a royal visit. They might mention trumpet fanfares, the National Anthem, soldiers, carriages, a special carpet, people bowing. All of these things, and the clothes, are signs that someone special – a royal person – is there.

Core material

In the play, Jesus was entering Jerusalem. To Christians, this was a royal visit, because they believe that Jesus is the special King whom God had promised to send to his people. They believe that Jesus is their King, and that when they become his friends, they become members of his kingdom. Many people at the time thought that Jesus was someone special. They gave him a special welcome, just as a royal person would get a special welcome if they came to your town today. But when the people of Jerusalem saw Jesus, they must have been surprised. He was riding a donkey, an animal used by poor people. He did not have a special carpet put down, only the cloaks and palm branches the people threw onto the road. Jesus was not staying in the best hotel in the city, or in the palace or a rich house. He was staying with his friends, and was just another of the people who had also come to Jerusalem for the Feast.

The Jewish people had been waiting for God's special king, the Messiah, for many years. Many of them thought that Jesus was the Messiah when they heard of the amazing things he had done. When they heard he was coming to Jerusalem, they thought that he would fight against the Romans who had defeated them. They longed for the Romans to leave their country, and to be free at last. But Jesus had a different message. He told people how they could become friends with God. Listening to God and doing what he wanted was the most important thing in the world, he told them. They began to realise that he was not going to attack the Romans. Yet when they saw him riding into Jerusalem on a donkey, some of them remembered some words which had been written many, many years before by one of God's prophets: 'Be joyful, Jerusalem!... Look! Your King is coming to you... gentle and riding on a donkey' (Zechariah 9:9).

Jesus' enemies were worried as they watched the crowds welcoming Jesus. Something would have to be done: he was too popular!

Prayer/Reflection

He could have come into the city as the King of the people,

With rich robes and bowing servants.

But he came in as God's King,

A man on a donkey,

Bringing a message of God's love.

OR

The people who expected Jesus to attack the Romans had not understood him at all. They hadn't listened to the whole story. Are we sometimes too quick to decide what someone is like? Do you need to listen to the whole story about someone at the moment?

Music suggestions

- We have a King who rides a donkey, 264, *Junior Praise*
- Trotting, trotting, 128, *The Complete Come and Praise*
- Praise King Jesus, 143, *Children's Praise*

Background notes

- The Jewish people had been expecting the promised Messiah for centuries. They saw him as a warrior king, who would liberate them from the Romans. Most of them could not reconcile these expectations with the realities of Jesus' life and death. Many turned against him during Holy Week because of this. When he entered the city, the crowd called out 'Hosanna', which means 'Save now'; they also called him the Son of David – it was prophesied that the Messiah would be a descendant of King David. Palm leaves were associated with royalty and with celebrations.
- Jerusalem was crowded, as many people had come there as usual for the Feast of the Passover.
- The Jewish leaders were probably jealous of Jesus' popularity, and frightened by the sight and sound of the crowd welcoming him. If this developed into a riot or demonstration, the Roman soldiers would be called in to deal with it from their headquarters near the temple, and the leaders themselves would be in trouble. The Romans would be sensitive to the possibility of trouble. Roman rule was extremely unpopular, largely because of the religious differences between the two peoples.

Sketch: THE COURTYARD

CHARACTERS

PETER

CHORUS 1 (C 1)

CHORUS 2 (C 2)

PETER: It was cold in the courtyard.
I wandered over to the fire.
Jesus must have wished he could do the same –
It was a chilly night.

C 1: No one can know me here.

PETER: But I wasn't taking any chances –
I kept my head down,
Looked no one in the eye.
But a woman noticed me –
Just a poor servant girl.

C 2: Aren't you one of them – his friends – the prisoner's friends?

C 1: No, No! Not me! I don't even know him!

PETER: It was out so quickly, I couldn't stop myself!
I couldn't believe I'd said it!
It couldn't have been me speaking!
But now I was nervous.
How could she have known me?
How many others knew me?
I soon found out!

C 2: I know you – you're one of his friends!

PETER: I didn't recognise her –
Just another young woman.
But before I could stop myself,
I'd said it again…

C 1: No! I don't know him!

PETER: I was sick with shame!
The friend I loved the most!
But now I was really frightened.
Petrified!
They had Jesus,
And I guessed what they wanted to do with him.
Then, before I could even think,
It happened a third time…

C 2: You're one of his friends!
You're a Galilean!
You must know him.

C 1: No! I don't know the man!

PETER: And then I heard the cock crow –
Piercing the low voices.
And at that moment
My eyes met his –
Across the flames.
I thought he was angry with me,
But no.
His eyes showed only pity –
Pity for a poor, stupid, frightened man.
Me!
I couldn't face him any more.
I pushed my way outside
And cried.
I cried for Jesus –
And for my shame!

Assembly: THE COURTYARD

Theme: *Failure and forgiveness*

This story can be found in Luke 22:54–62.

Introduction

(*This introduction tells briefly what happened before the action of the play. If wished, it could be read before the play itself is watched.*)

It was the Passover, the time to remember how God had rescued the Jewish people from slavery in Egypt. Jesus ate this special meal with his disciples. He confused them by saying he was about to leave them. He said that all of them would abandon him to his enemies. Peter was horrified. 'Of course I won't leave you! I'll stay with you even if it means I get killed!' he said. Jesus replied, 'Peter, you say you will die to keep me safe. I tell you that you will say you don't even know me three times before the cockerel crows to tell us it is morning.' Then Jesus and his friends went to a quiet garden where he often spent time talking to God. There soldiers arrested him, guided by Judas, who had been one of his disciples. Jesus was dragged off to the High Priest's house, and questioned for hours as they tried to trick him into saying something they could kill him for. Peter followed secretly; he was too scared to help Jesus. He crept into the courtyard of the house.

Core material

Peter said that he would stay with Jesus whatever happened. He was with his friends, in a safe room. It was easy to say that he would be brave. But in the lonely, dark garden, with armed men arresting his friend, Peter did not feel so brave. He forgot his promises, and hid. Later, he waited in the courtyard to see what was going to happen. He felt safe at first. He thought no one knew him and that they didn't know he was one of Jesus' friends. When he found out that they did know who he was, he panicked again. He told them he had never met Jesus. When he heard the cockerel, he remembered what Jesus had said, and he was heartbroken.

We can be like Peter. It is very easy to sound brave when we are with friends. But when we are by ourselves, it is not so easy! Sometimes, we seem to be like two different people – just as Peter did. But Jesus understood how Peter felt. After he had died and had then risen to life again, Jesus met Peter. Jesus didn't say, 'Right, that's it, Peter. You had your chance, and you failed.' He gave Peter a chance to say sorry for what he had done, and then told him that he still wanted him to do the special job he had given him before. Jesus had chosen Peter to be one of the most important leaders of his friends. Perhaps when our friends let us down, we could think about Peter and about ourselves.

Prayer/Reflection

Peter wasn't perfect – and neither are we! We can all make promises and then fail to keep them. We make mistakes and need to be forgiven, just as Jesus forgave Peter for his mistakes. Think about it – do we want people to forgive us when we do something wrong, or do we want them to keep on reminding us? How do we treat others when they let us down?

Music suggestions

- Feed my lambs, 34, *A Year of Celebration*
- Forgive me, God, 31, *Children's Praise*

Background notes

- The watch between midnight and 3 am was known as 'cock crow' to the Romans. Luke's account suggests that an actual cockerel was heard.
- Peter was right to be frightened, as the authorities could easily have decided to get rid of Jesus' close followers too.

Sketch: THE CENTURION'S TALE

CHARACTERS

CENTURION (CENT)
CHORUS 1 (C 1)
CHORUS 2 (C 2)

CENT: Crucifixions!
Don't tell me about them!
I'm a centurion, so
I've seen hundreds of them!
Well, it's my job, isn't it?
All part and parcel of the daily duties of a centurion of the Imperial Army.
But he was different, this Jesus,
Different in every way.
I mean, all the other men we crucified were criminals –
Thieves, murderers, terrorists.
You name them, we crucified them!
But, as I said, Jesus was different.
I could see that from the moment I first saw him.
He was quiet, calm;
You might almost say he was at peace with himself.
But my job is to crucify them,
Not judge them.
Now the priests were saying…

C 1: This man is guilty of treason.

CENT: They were clever!
They knew the emperor wouldn't like that!
So Pilate asked him…

C 2: Are you the King of the Jews?

CENT: Instead of jabbering on like all the others,
Jesus was silent!
He wouldn't reply –
Not a word.
He wouldn't play their game!
So Pilate asked…

C 1: What shall I do with this man?

C 2: Crucify him!

CENT: I hate crowds.
They're all so brave when they gang up together!

C 1: Then I wash my hands of the matter!

CENT: Said Pilate.
Then my job really began.
Now, I'm a hard man.
I don't usually blink an eyelid when I have a man flogged.
But this time, as I said, it was different.
Flogging is nearly as bad as crucifixion,
And this gentle man did not deserve either!
I was sorry, really sorry, I had to do it!
And it left him weak –
Half dead!
The poor man could not carry his cross – he was so weak by now.
So I hauled someone out of the crowd –
A Cyrenian, they said, called Simon.

C 2: Carry the cross for the prisoner,
And look sharp about it!

CENT: He carried it –
Right up to Skull Hill –
What a horrible place! –
And there we crucified him
With two thieves!
What an insult!
Crucifixion was bad enough,
But between two common criminals?
But even then he was different!
He spoke kindly to one of the thieves.

And he had time for his mother!

C 1: Mother, John will be your son. He will look after you.

C 2: John, my mother will be your mother. Look after her!

CENT: Unbelievable!
In all his agony, he was worried about other people!
Mind you, the crowds had no pity for him.
I told you I hate crowds.
They were mocking him –
Especially those priests.
They must have hated him.

C 1: If you are the Son of God, come down from that cross!

CENT: And…

C 2: He saved others, so let's see him save himself!

CENT: What a cruel joke!
But then the sky turned black.
They didn't like that.
And Jesus –
I could see he was going –
Cried out words of forgiveness.
I couldn't believe my ears!

C 2: Father, forgive them,
They don't understand.

CENT: They usually die cursing,
Not praying!
But now he was sinking fast.
His last words I couldn't understand –
Something about…

C 1: It is finished!

CENT: What was finished?
I'd like to know.
He was like no one I had ever met before!
God?
Who knows what he is like?
But yes, if anyone was the Son of God…

C 2: Surely this man was the Son of God!

CENT: It's the only way I can understand it!
But, do you know, his enemies still hadn't finished with him.
I let his friends take down his body,
They wrapped him in cloth and took him away
To a cave.
But, even then,
The priests insisted on a stone being put across the cave,
And an armed guard!
I wonder what they thought would happen?

Assembly: THE CENTURION'S TALE

THEME: *Jesus' death*

This story can be found in Matthew 27:11–44; Luke 22:63 – 23:49; John 18:28 – 19:30.

Introduction

For three years, Jesus had travelled around the towns and villages of Palestine, teaching the people and helping them. People learned what he was like by watching him at work. When they saw him talking to women and children as well as to men, they knew that he thought women and children were as important as men. Not everyone thought this at the time. When they saw Jesus healing people with many different illnesses, they knew that he was powerful and that he cared about people. When they saw him spending time with people who had done wrong things, and helping them and forgiving them, they knew that he loved them and wanted them to be his friends. When they saw him making a few loaves and fishes into enough food for thousands of people, they knew that he was so powerful that the normal laws of nature did not apply to him. When they listened to his teaching about God, they learned that God loved them. Christians believe that while Jesus was dying on the cross, he was still showing the people what he was like.

Core material

The people had seen Jesus do amazing things. Some of them probably realised that he could have saved himself from the cross at any time. Christians believe that it was his love for his friends which took him to the cross and kept him on it, not the soldiers and their nails. The things Jesus said also tell us about him. Recap with the pupils: he was kind to one of the thieves who was dying with him; he thought about his own mother and made sure that John would look after her; he asked God to forgive the very people who were killing him. Discuss with the pupils what each of these show us about Jesus. Then he shouted, 'It is finished!' This was not a cry of defeat but of victory. It means that a job has been completed. Christians believe that Jesus had done what he came to earth to do. He had died for the people he loved. Christians believe that the wrong things people do separate them from God. Jesus had done nothing wrong, but he died for the things others had done wrong, as if he had done them himself. He took the punishment for them, so now, Christians believe, God can forgive people for the things they have done wrong, and people can become God's friends.

Prayer/Reflection

Thank you, Jesus, that you were willing to die so that people could become friends with God.
OR
If people can find out what we are like from what we say, what do they learn about you from what you say?

Music suggestions

Were you there?, 94, *A Year of Celebration*

Background notes

- A centurion was an officer in the Roman army.
- What the centurion said is variously conveyed as, 'Son of God', 'a son of God' or 'a righteous man'. He was trying to convey his sense that this man was different.
- Crucifixion was widely used by the Romans, mainly to keep the Provinces in control, and they admitted it was a brutal death. The Jews were forbidden, under Roman rule, to carry out the death penalty, so they had to take Jesus before Pilate, the Roman Governor. He was in Jerusalem with his troops on hand in case of trouble at the Passover. Herod was in Jerusalem for the Passover, too. As the Romans' puppet king, he had the right to try Jesus.
- Care should always be taken to avoid giving the impression that all Jews opposed Jesus. He and his disciples were all Jews. His enemies among the Jews opposed him for several reasons, but racial prejudice was not one of them.

NOTE: The crucifixion is a difficult subject to deal with. The pupils may well raise questions which an individual teacher, for any reason, will not feel able to answer. This can lead to discussion, or to the pupils contacting someone in the local community to find out their thoughts about the issue, for instance. Not knowing all the answers is not a failure on our part.

Sketch: FIRST LIGHT

CHARACTERS

MARY

CHORUS 1 (C 1)

CHORUS 2 (C 2)

MARY: So Jesus was dead!
It was so hard for us, his closest friends –
The waiting, I mean. It was so hard.
You see, it was the Sabbath Day.
From sunset on Friday evening
Till sunset on Saturday…

C 1: You will do no work.

MARY: And then it was too dark to do anything.
All we wanted to do was to put precious ointment on his body –
It was the custom to do that for a loved one.
We just had to wait for Sunday morning.
Jesus' body was in the tomb.
We had the ointment ready.
All that love we wanted to pour out on him!
It was the least we could do.
But we just had to wait.

C 2: You will do no work on the Sabbath Day.

MARY: Well, by Sunday morning, we were nearly at bursting point.
By the time the sun's first rays had appeared,
We were up and ready.
Now, at last, we could do it,
Our last act of love for him!
He had loved us,
And now we could show our love for him.
If only we had done more while he was alive!
So down to his tomb we went,
We women who had followed him everywhere,
Down to his last resting-place –
Or so we thought!
The cave in the hillside,
Where they put his body two long days ago.
Where they had rolled the stone across.
Our only worry was how we would get in.
Who would be about at that early hour
To roll the stone aside for us?
We needn't have worried about that.
But nothing could have prepared us for the shock.
It was open!
The cave, I mean.
The stone was rolled aside
And inside was a figure dressed in white.
I can't describe him,
But I'll always remember his words…

C 1: Don't be afraid!
You're looking for Jesus, aren't you?
He's not here! He's alive!
Go and tell his friends.

MARY: We didn't wait a moment!
We were off, running as fast as we could,
Back to the city.
Back to find the others – the disciples.
We burst in on them,
Sad and lonely, and told them.
There was no stopping them – Peter and John!
They left us behind, they ran so fast!

It was John who got there first.
He looked in.
There were the strips of cloth from his body,
And the cloth that had covered his head.
Then Peter caught up with him
And they went in.
It was odd!
The cloth was lying just as it had been –
But there was no body in it!
Was it true that Jesus had come back to life –
Just as he had said he would?
So off they dashed to tell the others.
But I couldn't go away.
It was too good to be true.
What if the soldiers had taken the body away?
Then there were two figures dressed in white.

C 1: Why are you crying?

MARY: They asked.

C 2: They've taken Jesus away!

MARY: I replied.
And then there was someone behind me – the gardener, I supposed.
He might know where Jesus was!

C 1: Sir, please sir, do you know where they have taken him?

MARY: He just said…

C 2: Mary!

MARY: It was him! I'd know his voice anywhere!
Now I knew that he was alive! I just said…

C 1: Teacher!

Assembly: FIRST LIGHT

THEME: *Jesus' resurrection*

This story can be found in Luke 24:1–12 and John 20:1–18.

You will need:

an empty box attractively wrapped as a present; a suitable 'consolation' prize, such as an orange or a bar of chocolate

Introduction

NOTE: Arrange with a colleague beforehand to be the recipient of the parcel, but do not tell them it is empty: think up a suitable reason for them to receive a small present from you or from the school – for instance, supervising a wall display for the corridor, or leading the singing the previous day.

Show the pupils the parcel, and invite one or two to guess what is in it. Explain who it is for and why. Invite that person to open the parcel in front of the pupils, explaining that they have been looking forward to it since you told them about it. When they have found out it is empty, ask them how they feel. Give them the 'consolation' prize.

Core material

Finding the box to be empty was a great disappointment. In the play, the women found that the cave was empty, and at first they were disappointed, because they had hoped to be able to anoint Jesus' body as a sign of their love. The women's feelings when they arrived at the tomb were like a picture of how all the disciples were feeling. They had all been Jesus' friends. They had travelled and worked with him for three years. They had probably imagined that he would be with them for many more years. But suddenly he was taken from them and was cruelly killed. Now, they didn't know what to do. They were too frightened to be seen out in the streets. They were hiding away in a friend's house. They didn't know whether they should return to their homes or not. They were confused. Their lives must have seemed empty and disappointing, like the box. But then the women found out that the empty tomb was not really a disappointment. It was a sign that something far greater and better than they had expected had happened. Jesus was alive! Soon, the other disciples discovered this too. Jesus gave them a surprise present – himself!

Prayer/Reflection

Thank you for the great surprise of that first Easter. Thank you that the tomb was empty, because Jesus was alive again.

Music suggestions

- Now the green blade rises, 174, *Junior Praise*; 107, *A Year of Celebration*
- All in an Easter garden, 130, *The Complete Come and Praise*
- Three ladies are walking, 175, *Children's Praise*
- He is risen, 59, *Children's Praise*
- Touch your toes, 176, *A Year of Celebration*

Background notes

- It was customary for bodies to be anointed with a mixture of spices at burial, which was usually on the same day as death. There had been no time for the women to do this at Jesus' burial because he had to be buried before the Sabbath started at sunset on the Friday. (The Sabbath lasts until sunset on Saturday.) Tombs were usually caves, natural or man-made. Jesus was buried in the tomb that Joseph of Arimathea had prepared for himself.
- By this time, most Jewish people believed in resurrection, but the Sadducees did not. Christians do believe in it. The writers of the Gospels include several details to show readers of the time that Jesus was actually alive again, and not a 'ghost' or a revived person. He ate in front of witnesses and invited Thomas to touch him. The resurrection of Jesus is a central tenet of Christian faith. Christians believe that it shows he has defeated all that evil could do. He conquered death and Christians believe that, as a result, they too will be raised to eternal life.

SECTION 2: PUPPET PLAYS

Using puppets in school

Based on notes by Jon Webster

I am an inheritor of a proud tradition. I can visualise Neanderthal men and women entertaining their children on dark nights with shadow puppets in the firelight at the back of draughty caves. Maybe even then puppet shows were part of religious ceremonies. Certainly puppetry has a very real part today in some religious traditions, and not just for children. For me, puppets and the stories they bring to life are part of my effort to make known the stories of Jesus, and to tell them in a way that will make them relevant to the current generation. So many children nowadays have a negative attitude, based on almost total ignorance, towards anything Christian. I have developed a range of puppets and scripts to use with children, in my attempts to conquer this ignorance.

I use many sorts of puppets: glove, stick, string – even wooden spoon and dishmop! I also use shadow puppets, using the medium of the overhead projector. This use is not always easy: it is difficult for one pair of hands to whip shadow puppets off and on the projector at the necessary speed, but pupils can provide help.

Puppetry is a way of 'doing drama' which gives an element of control, as it is within a firm framework. It can be a means of meeting the Listening and Speaking – and, if you wish, the Writing – elements of the National Curriculum English requirements. The class can work in pairs on such tasks as:

a) drawing and developing characters;
b) writing notes on how characters would behave, move, talk, etc;
c) writing rough drafts of new scripts;
d) editing scripts;
e) making the puppets (using skills developed in Art and Technology);
f) rehearsing and performing plays.

Younger pupils and those requiring special help could omit the written stages. It has been noteworthy, however, that puppets can evoke a valuable response in Special Needs pupils. It is an area of work in which they can shine, being a means of communication not reliant on reading and writing. A puppet can provide some pupils with a welcome 'screen' to hide behind until they are ready to emerge as themselves.

Pupils love making and using puppets. For ideas to get a class started on this see page 66.

Puppetry also has potential for PSE work. Cooperation is called for in the production and presentation. Also, the subject matter of stories based on Jesus' parables or on stories about biblical characters, is about human behaviour and its deepest motivations.

You do not need professionally made puppets to benefit from the learning experience that puppetry offers. Neither do the puppets need to be made of expensive materials. It is the joint enthusiasm of yourself and the pupils, teamwork and a bit of creativity thrown in, that will make your project a success. Such a project can be a learning experience for the pupils and the teacher. Bible stories can be an obvious starting point for puppetry: simple but penetrating stories whose humour is used to reach out to our humanity. Jesus' parables are extremely useful and can give rise to much discussion. As the culture of Jesus' Palestine is stripped away, the pupils will discover the vitality of Jesus' preaching. It is one way to bring the Bible alive to a generation better acquainted with computers and videos than with everyday life in the Middle East. Puppetry is the ideal way both to learn and to present these stories to the rest of the school.

I believe that the story is more important than the puppets. Puppets are just the means to the end of telling the story.

Puppetry should not be turned into a chore! It will be most effective when both the teacher and the pupils are enjoying it. Start with simple puppets and simple stories. You will find that the pupils will modify your ideas and make them – and the puppets – uniquely their own.

Puppetry is storytelling with a visual 'bait'. Children, in this age of television and video, seem to need something visual to centre their attention while they listen. But a puppet show is also a 'live' experience, shared by both audience and participants. My own shows have worked best when I have been able to develop plenty of audience participation. This could be achieved by the puppets asking the audience simple questions during the action. (These have not been included, but can easily be ad libbed as you work.) Children love to believe in the drama they are watching – we just need to give them the opportunity.

Keep your shows short and 'crisp', with plenty of action.

I hope you will soon be trying out these ideas and scripts, and that you will be able to develop your own shows with the pupils and devise new puppets to make. You will find that the drama scripts and the puppet play scripts are largely interchangeable between the two sections: it is easy to adapt a sketch for presentation as a puppet play, and vice versa.

SIMPLE PUPPETS TO MAKE IN THE CLASSROOM

Based on Jon Webster's ideas

NOTE: Not all of the stages in making the puppets are suitable or safe for the pupils to carry out themselves. Materials also need to be chosen with care. Constant reference should be made to the teacher's Health and Safety Regulations.

YOU WILL NEED THESE ITEMS FOR MOST OF THE PUPPETS:

sticky tape
felt-tip pens
scraps of fabric and felt
coloured cellophane (or sweet wrappers)
string
card, such as cereal boxes
safe adhesive suitable for paper, card and fabric
wool, thread, etc for hair
smooth garden canes
florists' wire

FINGER PUPPET

Make a template

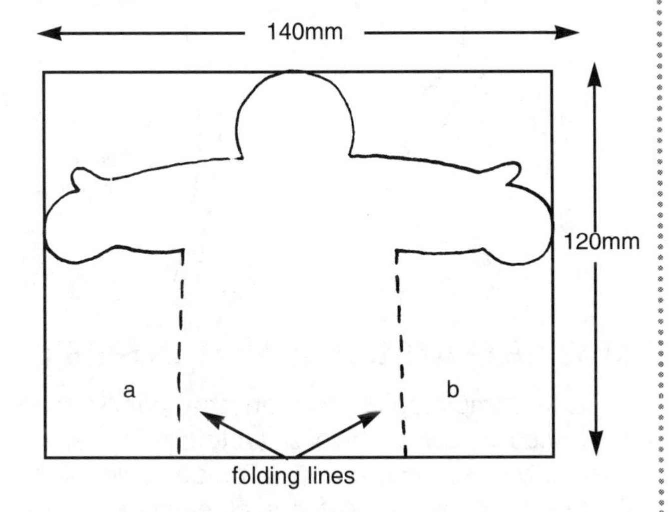

1 Use your template to cut out the puppet from card. (cut solid lines only)
2 Fold a and b and stick with tape at the back of the puppet to form a tubular shape.
3 Give the puppet a character with felt-tip pens and fabric.

HAND PUPPET

This is made in the same way as the finger puppet, but is based on a larger template, so that a pupil's whole hand can be inserted inside the puppet. Make your template about 225mm high and 220mm wide. Legs could then be fixed onto the bottom edge at the front of the puppet's 'body'.

WALKING FINGER PUPPET

Make a template (see top of next page)
1 Using the template, cut out the puppet from card.
2 Cut out the finger holes, adjusting the size to the user's fingers. (pupils will need help with this)
3 Use fabric and felt-tip pens to personalise the puppet.

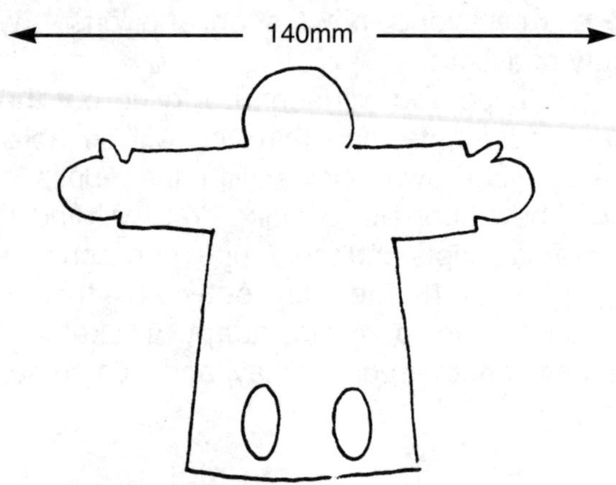

STICK PUPPET

These are traditionally operated with three sticks. This version uses two.

1 Make a hand puppet, but with only one arm.
2 Attach a length of string to the armless shoulder.

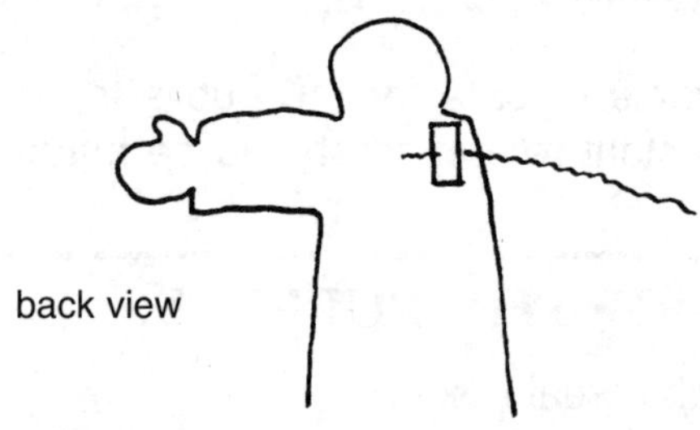

3 Cut two rectangles of card, colour them to match the puppet's body, roll them into tubes, and secure them with sticky tape. Thread them onto the string to make the two sections of the arm.

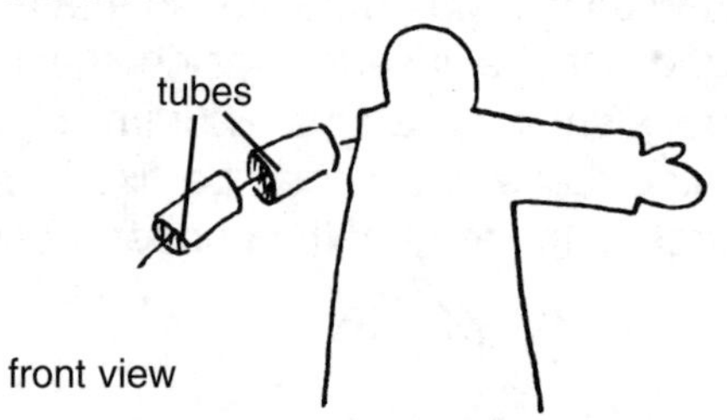

4 Cut out a double hand, using the template, and colour it. Fold it to form a hand, and sticky tape it to the end of the string. A cane can then be secured to the hand by sticky tape if necessary. The second cane supports the body.

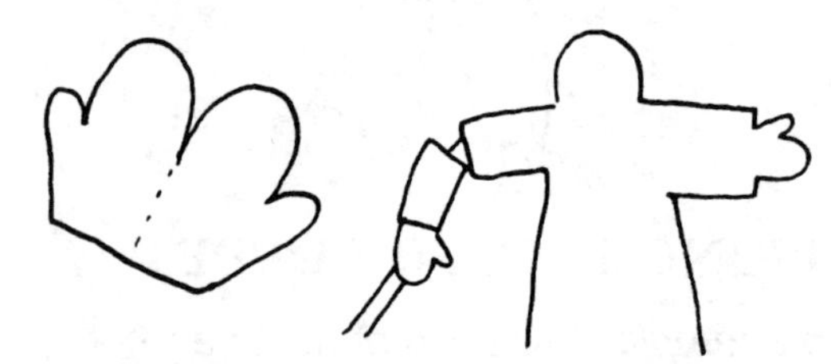

WOODEN SPOON PUPPET

You will need:
a wooden spoon

1 Facial features are drawn and coloured on the back of a wooden spoon. Felt or wool can be used for hair.
2 If wanted, a cardboard body shape can be decorated and stuck onto the handle of the spoon, leaving space for the user's hand.

DISHMOP PUPPET

You will need:
a piece of sponge or a foam ball
a dishmop

1 Use felt-tip pens or pieces of felt to make a face on the sponge or ball.
2 The teacher can then cut a hole through the sponge or ball so that the handle of the dishmop can be pushed through, from the top of the head. The cotton fibres then form the hair.

3 A cardboard body can be made and stuck onto the handle.

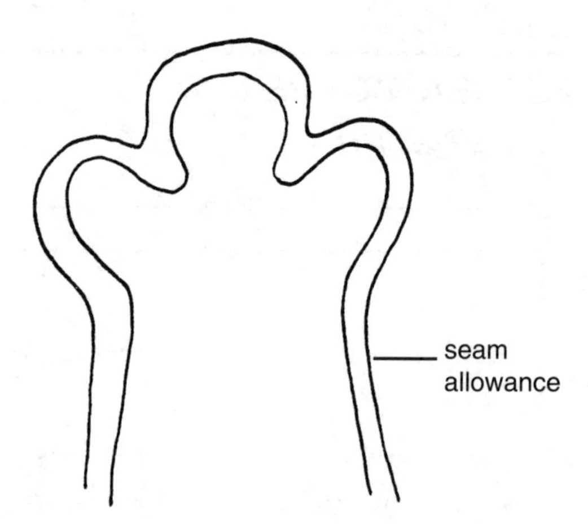

MATERIAL/FELT HAND PUPPET

1 Use templates based on the pupils' own hands to cut out two suitably sized shapes, using the picture as a guide. Allowance needs to be made for a glueing or sewing border, and for ease of movement.
2 Decorate one piece as the front of the puppet's body.
3 Glue or sew the pieces together.
4 If wished, a face can be made out of cardboard to stick on the head shape, instead of decorating the fabric itself. Wool can be used as hair.
5 Similarly, cardboard hands can be cut out and glued to the ends of the arms.

COAT-HANGER PUPPET

You will need:
wire coat-hanger, with trouser bar
a square of fabric – about 330–350 mm square

1 Make a cardboard face and hands, decorate them, and glue them to the fabric as shown.

2 Sticky tape lengths of strong thread to the back of the face and hands. (Coins taped to these three points will help the puppet to keep in shape.)
3 Attach the threads to the hanger.

This puppet is limited in movement, but is a useful addition to some plays.

NOTES

FACES

1 An alternative to simple, drawn facial features is to use coloured cellophane stuck on the back of the puppet, over pre-cut holes for mouth and eyes.

2 With any of these puppets, a 3D effect can be easily achieved by:
i) making a face of the correct size out of cardboard;
ii) sticking a matchbox on the original face of the puppet, and then attaching the new face on top of this.

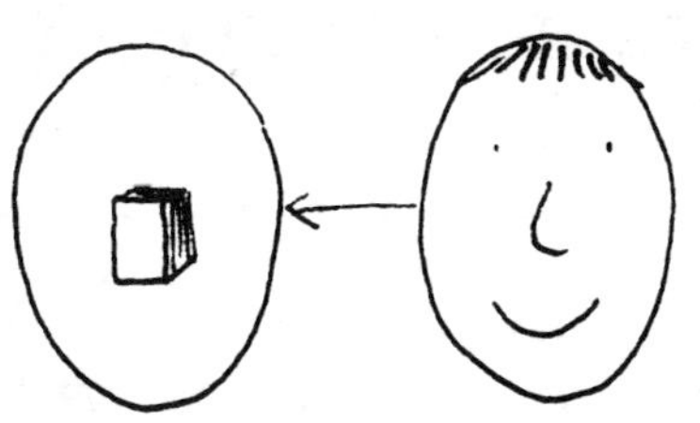

3 A more realistic nose for cardboard faces can be achieved by making one using a template, and inserting the tabs of this in slits cut into the face.

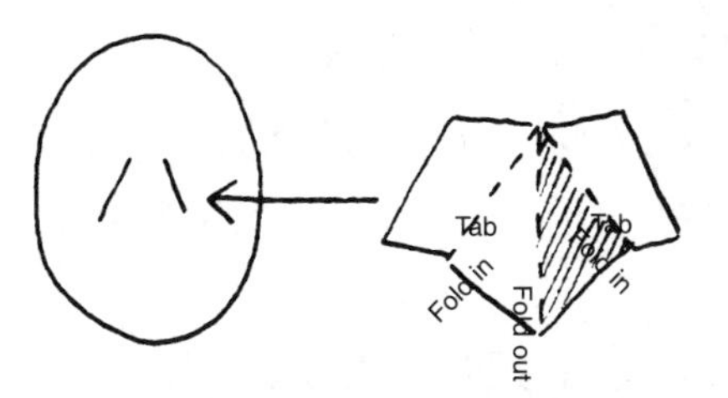

VARIETY

Puppets can be made using a mixture of ideas from different puppets listed here. Each play can also employ a variety of types of puppets, matched for size except when differences of size are used for dramatic effect.

PROPS

Various props can be invented for the plays, using the pupils' imagination. For instance, the flames of the furnace in 'Firewalkers' can be strips of red and yellow crepe paper attached to a garden cane.

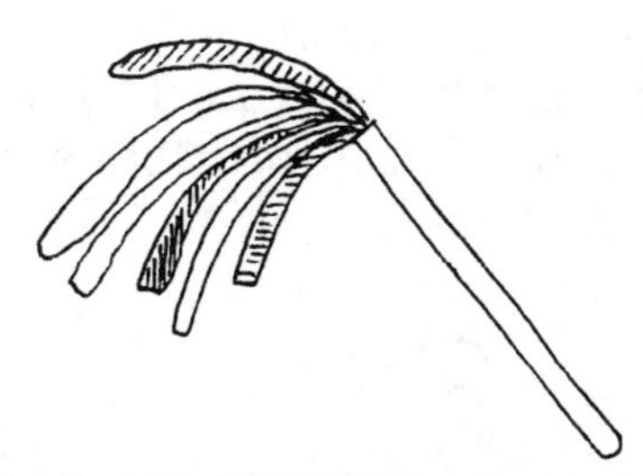

SHADOW PUPPETS

The use of shadow puppets is well-established in both amateur and professional situations. The simplest way to use this form of puppetry in the classroom or in assembly is by utilising the overhead projector.

You will need:
acetate sheets
OHP pens
cardboard, eg from cereal boxes
glue suitable for card and acetate sheets, suitable for use on overhead projector
florists' wire
coloured cellophane or coloured clear wrappers from sweets

ACETATE SHEET PUPPETS

The obvious 'puppets' to use are simply figures drawn with OHP pens on acetate sheets. If more than one figure features in a scene, each can be drawn on a separate sheet, preferably in a corner. Some movement can then be introduced by moving the sheet(s).

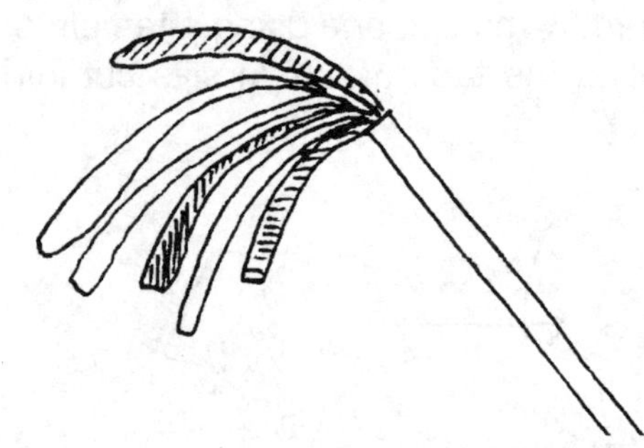

SILHOUETTE PUPPETS

1 Cut simple outlines from card. Remind the pupils that the puppets will only be seen in profile.

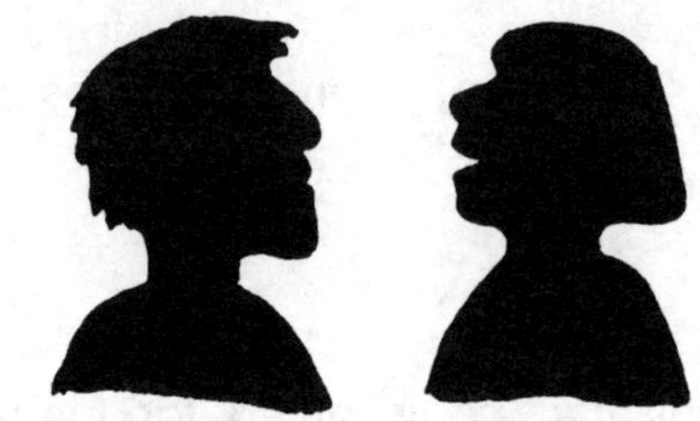

EITHER

2 Stick the puppets onto the sheets, and use as above.

OR

3 Stick a garden cane onto its feet, to move the puppet over the screen.
4 This idea can be developed by giving each puppet one or more movable limbs, using paper fasteners.

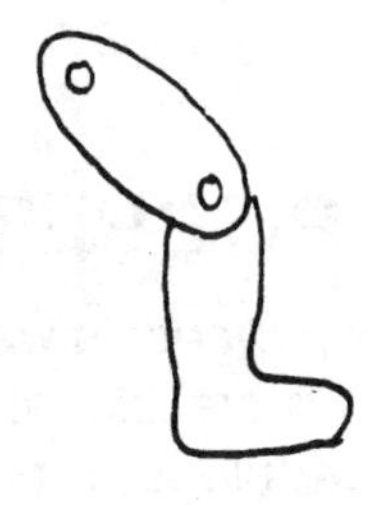

The limbs can be operated by a lever of florists' wire.

COLOURED OVERHEAD PUPPETS

1 Draw a simple outline of the required puppet on card.

2 Draw another line within the outline, and then cut out the middle, leaving a 'frame' of card.
3 Glue this frame onto a sheet of acetate, and colour the area inside the frame appropriately.

If you cannot afford to use acetate sheets, fill in the frame of the puppet with cellophane sweet wrappers.

TITLE AND BACKGROUND

PAGES

Title pages can be designed, and background scenes produced on acetate. If necessary, these can be traced from books. If a scene is changed during a story, the new scene should be slid over the old one before it is removed, so that the screen is not left blank.

SPECIAL EFFECTS

Moving backgrounds can be created – for such things as fire or the sea – by using two or more sheets which are then moved independently. Fire would need sheets of red, orange and yellow flames, and sea sheets of blue and green waves. Coloured cellophane, secured in a double card frame (as with the puppets above), could substitute for one sheet of acetate.

(For bibliography see page 95.)

OLD TESTAMENT PUPPET PLAYS

Puppet play: FIRE-WALKERS

CHARACTERS

NARRATOR 1 (N 1)
NARRATOR 2 (N 2)
KING
SHADRACH (SHAD)
MESHACH (MESH)
ABEDNEGO (ABED)

N 1: Once, in ancient Babylon...

N 2: ... there was a mighty king.

N 1: One day the king ordered his men to build a huge statue...

N 2: ... of one of his gods.

N 1: It was ninety feet high...

N 2: ... and made of gold.

N 1: Everyone was ordered to come and see it...

N 2: ... and they all obeyed.

N 1: Then the king gave orders...

KING: When my musicians play with pipes and lyre and harp, everyone – everyone! – must bow down and worship the statue of my god.

N 2: The musicians played... and everyone bowed down to the statue...

N 1: ... everyone except...

N 2: ... three Jewish men called...

N 1: ... Shadrach, Meshach and Abednego.

N 2: The king was furious!

KING: Do you refuse to worship the statue of my god? I shall have you flung into the burning, fiery furnace!

N 1: The men replied...

SHAD: Our God is able to save us – even from the burning, fiery furnace!

MESH: But, even if he doesn't, we will not worship any other god!

ABED: We will not bow to the statue!

SHAD: We will not worship it!

MESH: We are Jews!

ABED: We worship the true God!

N 2: The king was so angry that he gave orders...

KING: Make the fire seven times hotter! Now throw Shadrach, Meshach and Abednego into the white-hot centre of the fire!

N 1: Now the king rubbed his eyes. He couldn't believe what he saw!

KING: Shadrach, Meshach and Abednego, servants of the most high God, come out! Why, the flames haven't touched your clothes – or even singed a hair of your heads! Who has saved these brave men? Your God sent his angel to save you because you would not worship any god but him. No other god could do that!

N 2: Then he turned to his people.

KING: The God of Shadrach, Meshach and Abednego is a great God. Let no one say a word against the God of Shadrach, Meshach and Abednego.

Director's note.

Two narrators have been used instead of one to try to give the piece more variety and rhythm. If you wish, they can be represented by two additional puppets, one on each side of the stage.

ASSEMBLY: FIRE-WALKERS

THEME: *witnesses of God*

This is based on the story of the three friends in the fiery furnace, which can be found in Daniel 3:1–30.

Introduction

Shadrach, Meshach and Abednego were Jews who had been taken from their own country to live as palace servants in Babylon, a big city in a different country far from home. You might think that the three friends had lost everything – their homes, their families and their country. Even their names were not their own names! The man who looked after them in the palace had given them new Babylonian names. But the three friends had not lost everything. They still had God as their friend. They knew that he was still with them, even though their people had done so many wrong things that God had allowed them to be taken to Babylon. These friends still loved God, and wanted to obey his laws. God had commanded his people not to worship any other god but him, so when Shadrach, Meshach and Abednego were ordered by the king to worship the great statue, they were bound to get into trouble.

Core material

It would have been easy for the three to avoid their terrible punishment. They were good workers, and Nebuchadnezzar gave them another chance to bow down to the statue. But they still refused to save themselves. They said, 'God can rescue us even from your furnace. But if he doesn't choose to rescue us, we will still not bow down to your god.' They did not know whether God would rescue them. They just knew that he could if he wanted to. They knew that they couldn't command God to save them but they trusted him and refused to give in. Ask the pupils what the Babylonians would have said if they had saved themselves. They might have got the impression that the friends thought God was not worth risking their own lives for: he couldn't be the great and loving God they had said he was. But when God saved them, the Babylonians saw for themselves that God loved his people and that he was indeed very powerful.

The friends risked their lives to show the people what God was like and to stay faithful to him. People who do this and who die because of their belief in God are called 'martyrs'. This word means someone who 'witnesses' or tells people about what they have seen or know, just as a witness does in court. Christian martyrs witness to their belief in Jesus by dying for it. Shadrach, Meshach and Abednego were willing to become martyrs and to die. Because of this, when people saw them willing to die and God saving them, many of them learned what God was like for the first time.

Prayer

Thank you, Father, for the many people who have been willing to die rather than to give up following you.

OR

In this country, people are free to believe in what they like. But in some countries, people do not have this freedom. Think about your freedom today, and about the people who are told what they should do and believe all the time.

Music suggestions

- When the road is rough and steep, 279, *Junior Praise*
- Daniel and his friends, 18, *Children's Praise*
- Sometimes problems can be big, 461, *Junior Praise*; 154, *Children's Praise*

Background notes

- See notes on the exile, pages 74 and 75.
- When the exiles arrived in Babylon, they were given new names. For some reason, we know Shadrach, Meshach and Abednego by these new names, but although Daniel was given a new name too, we know him by his Hebrew name.

Puppet play: DANIEL

CHARACTERS

NARRATOR 1 (N 1)
NARRATOR 2 (N 2)
PLOTTER 1 (P 1)
PLOTTER 2 (P 2)
KING
FRIEND (F)
DANIEL (D)
SCRIBE

Director's notes

In this sketch, there are two narrators to give the play an added rhythm and authority. However, it can be performed with just one person reading both parts, if necessary. If you have two voices, you can have two puppets, one on each side of the stage all the way through the play to represent the two narrators.

The repetition in the play is intended to give rhythm.

N 1: Daniel was a Jew in Babylon, far from home.

N 2: But because he was clever and honest and hard-working…

N 1: … and because he was always faithful to God…

N 2: … he rose to become one of the king's chief ministers.

N 1: But because he was a Jew…

N 2: … and faithful to God…

N 1: … he made many enemies…

N 2: … and people were jealous of him.

P 1: Look, there goes Daniel – the king's favourite!

P 2: A Jew! *His* God is not *our* god! He is not one of *us*.

P 1: We must get rid of him!

P 2: But how? He is honest, hard-working and loyal to the king.

P 1: He never puts a foot wrong.

P 2: There must be something we can find against him!

P 1: We will set a trap.

N 1: Every day since he arrived in Babylon, Daniel had prayed to God…

N 2: … three times a day…

N 1: … kneeling at his open window…

N 2: … facing far-off Jerusalem.

P 1: Look, there he is again, praying to his God.

P 2: Not *our* god – *his* God.

P 1: And that is how we will trap him!

P 2: How?

P 1: Come with me to the king. I have a plan to get rid of Daniel – Daniel, who worships the foreign God.

N 1: So they went to the king…

N 2: … and said…

P 1: O King, live for ever! We have agreed on a new law: for thirty days, no one may ask anything from any god or man except Your Majesty.

P 2: Whoever breaks this law will be…

P 1: … thrown to the lions!

KING: Good! Scribe! Draw up this new law and then I shall sign it.

N 1: The new law was signed by the king.

N 2: It was read out to everyone in the country:

SCRIBE: No one is to pray to anyone but

the king for thirty days. The punishment for disobedience is to be thrown to the lions.

N 1: But Daniel continued to pray to God…

N 2: … three times a day…

N 1: … kneeling at his open window…

N 2: … facing far-off Jerusalem.

F: Daniel, Daniel, you will be seen praying to God. It is dangerous. If you are caught, no one can help you – not even the king.

D: Am I to stop praying to God? My friend, I am an old man now. I have been faithful to God all my life. I will not stop praying to him now – not for any law!

N 1: The plotters were delighted that Daniel continued to pray…

N 2: … three times a day…

N 1: … kneeling at his open window…

N 2: … facing far-off Jerusalem.

P 1: There is Daniel, praying to his God.

P 2: Our plot is working!

N 1: They went to the royal palace…

N 2: … and spoke to the king.

P 1: Daniel prays to *his* God…

P 2: … three times a day…

P 1: … kneeling at his open window…

P 2: … facing far-off Jerusalem.

P 1: He must be punished!

P 2: The law is clear!

P 1: He must be thrown to the lions!

P 2: The law allows nothing else!

N 1: Now the king saw that he had been tricked.

N 2: He wanted to pardon Daniel.

KING: Daniel is a loyal servant ! But I cannot save him! I cannot change the law!

N 1: He could do nothing.

P 1: The law says that Daniel must be thrown to the lions.

KING: Bring Daniel here!

N 1: The king was horrified.

N 2: But he was trapped by his own stupid, selfish law.

KING: May your God save you from the lions, Daniel. Take Daniel to the lions' den!

N 2: The king did not sleep a wink that night.

KING: May Daniel's God save him from the lions!

N 1: At first light the king hurried down to the lions' den.

N 2: He called out…

KING: Daniel, was your God able to save you?

N 2: He was amazed to hear Daniel's voice!

D: Yes, Your Majesty. The lions have not hurt me. God knows I am faithful to him and to you, so he closed the lions' mouths and they did not harm me.

KING: Set Daniel free at once! Now, throw to the lions the plotters who accused him. Daniel, your God has saved you because you trusted him. Now, it is my command that everyone in my kingdom should fear and respect Daniel's God, who saved him from the lions. He is God for ever!

ASSEMBLY: DANIEL

THEME: *Standing up for one's beliefs*

This play is based on the story of Daniel in the lions' den, which can be found in Daniel 6:1–28. The story of Daniel and his friends refusing the food, which is used below, is in Daniel 1:1–21.

Introduction

In the play, Daniel had to stand up for what he believed. Ask the pupils to stand up. Is that what we mean when we say someone stands up for what they believe in? Ask them to sit down again, and then discuss the meaning of the phrase as used here. It would probably help to introduce or ask for some examples of situations in which someone has to stand up for their beliefs. For instance: a vegetarian might have to explain their beliefs and/or keep on refusing to eat inappropriate food; a pupil might refuse to join in the bullying of another pupil. Standing up for beliefs always makes a person stand out! Other people notice when someone refuses to do the things they do, and when someone disagrees with them. It is not a safe or an easy thing to do. Daniel was in a strange land. The people of Babylon had defeated Daniel's people, the Jews, and had taken them to live in Babylon in exile. This meant that they were like slaves; they were owned by the people of Babylon. They had to do as they were told or they would be in trouble. But even before the events in the play happened, Daniel had shown that he was not willing just to keep his head down and stay out of trouble. Standing up for his belief in God was more important.

Core material

Soon after the exiles arrived in Babylon, some of them were chosen to serve the king in the royal palace. Among these were Daniel and his three friends, Shadrach, Meshach and Abednego. They lived in the palace, and were given the same rich food and wine as the king. But it was against the laws God had given to the Jews to eat some of this food, and some of it was so rich that Daniel and his friends realised that they would not stay healthy if they ate it. They were used to a diet of fresh vegetables and to water rather than wine. So they said that they would eat and drink nothing but vegetables and water. The man who looked after them was worried. 'If you become unhealthy because of this diet, I will be blamed,' he said. So Daniel and his friends said that they would eat vegetables for just ten days. Then, if they were unwell, they would eat the food the king had sent for them. The man agreed to this. At the end of the ten days the four friends were more healthy than the people who had been given the king's rich food and drink. So they were allowed to carry on eating the food they were used to.

Daniel and his friends knew that they might get into trouble for speaking out about the food – just as Daniel knew later on that continuing to pray to God would get him into trouble. They were living in such a dangerous situation that other people would probably expect them to do all they could to stay out of more trouble. Instead, they deliberately placed themselves in danger. Doing what God wanted them to do was more important to them than anything else. They decided to stand up for God and for their belief in him. But it wasn't easy or safe!

Prayer/Reflection

As we grow up, we often have to stand up for the things we believe are right. Very few of us will ever be in danger because we do this! But it is not easy to stand up like this when others are against us and are making fun of us. Think carefully: is there anything or anyone you should be standing up for? Or are you making life difficult for someone who is struggling to stand up for something? Think silently about what you believe you should do.

NOTE: There is another story about Daniel's three friends on page 70.

Music suggestions

Daniel was a man of prayer, 36, *Junior Praise*

Daniel and his friends, 18, *Children's Praise*

Background notes

- Daniel prayed kneeling, facing Jerusalem. Jews usually prayed standing with their arms raised.
- Daniel had risen to posts of responsibility because of his hard work and complete trustworthiness.
- The Jews were originally taken to Babylon by the Babylonians under Nebuchadnezzar. He was king during the 'food' and fiery furnace episodes. The Persians defeated the Babylonians, so the exiles changed hands. The Persian king during the lions' den episode was Darius. The Babylonians often used fire for executions, but fire was sacred to the Persians and could not be used in that way, so lions and other methods were used instead. The lions may have been kept in a dug pit, with an opening in the roof, or in an enclosure with an open top with a spectators' gallery around it. Lions were also kept for hunting.
- The Jews were forbidden by God to worship any images or other gods. Through all his years in exile, Daniel had never compromised his faith in God, and he would not do so now, even though his life was at risk.
- The Jews knew that the food they were offered might well have been offered to idols first.
- Darius wanted to save Daniel, but couldn't because, once made, the laws of the Persians could not be changed.

Puppet play: ESTHER

CHARACTERS

NARRATOR 1 (N 1)
NARRATOR 2 (N 2)
ESTHER
PLOTTER 1 (P 1)
PLOTTER 2 (P 2)
MORDECAI (MORD)
KING
HAMAN
HAMAN'S WIFE (WIFE)
SCRIBE

N 1: There was once, in the city of Shushan in Persia, a rich and powerful king called Xerxes.

N 2: But King Xerxes could be very cruel…

N 1: … and he had enemies…

N 2: … enemies who plotted to kill him.

P 1: Xerxes is our king, but we must get rid of him.

P 2: He will have to die!

N 1: But the plotters were overheard by a man called Mordecai.

N 2: Mordecai was a Jew.

MORD: I heard those men plotting against the king.

N 1: So Mordecai went to the king.

N 2: He warned him about the men who were planning to kill him. (*Whispers in the King's ear.*)

KING: Thank you for warning me, Mordecai. Scribe! Write down Mordecai's name in the palace records! He shall be rewarded.

N 1: But the king forgot all about Mordecai.

N 2: He was busy choosing a new queen.

N 1: And the queen he chose was Esther.

N 2: Now Esther was Mordecai's adopted daughter.

N 1: She was beautiful and kind and everyone loved her.

N 2: As soon as he saw her, the king fell in love with her and she was soon Queen Esther.

N 1: But Mordecai had a problem.

N 2: The king's Prime Minister was a rich and cruel man named Haman.

N 1: Haman walked about through the town and expected people to bow to him.

N 2: And every one bowed to him…

N 1: … except Mordecai!

HAMAN: Bow to me, Mordecai!

MORD: No, Haman! I am a Jew. I bow only to God!

N 2: Haman was furious!

N 1: He complained to his wife.

HAMAN: There is this Jew called Mordecai. He will not bow down to me. He says, 'Jews only bow to their God.' (*Sarcastically.*)

WIFE: Well, my husband, you are the Prime Minister. Do something about Mordecai!

HAMAN: Very well. I will!

N 2: So Haman went to the king. (*Bow.*)

HAMAN: Your Majesty, there is in this country a group of people who are not loyal to you. They do not obey your laws, O King, only their own.

KING: Who are they?

HAMAN: The Jews.

KING: Well, what do you propose to do about them, Haman? You are the Prime Minister!

HAMAN: Your Majesty, I propose that we choose a particular day, and on that day we order the governors of every province to kill all the Jews!

KING: Good! Take this ring and seal the orders to my governors with it – then they will see that the orders have my royal authority.

HAMAN: Thank you, Your Majesty.

KING: But how shall we choose the day to have the Jews killed, Haman?

HAMAN: Let us cast lots for it, Your Majesty.

KING: Excellent, see that it is done.

N 1: So they cast lots to choose the day when every Jew in Persia would be executed.

N 2: The Jewish people, of course, were terrified by the news.

N 1: They went into mourning.

N 2: They ate no food and cried out loud.

N 1: Mordecai rushed to see Queen Esther.

ESTHER: What is the matter, Mordecai?

MORD: You must go to the king and plead for our lives, Esther. Perhaps he will be merciful and let us live.

ESTHER: But I cannot do that, Mordecai. The king has not sent for me for a whole month. If I go to him without being summoned, he may have me executed!

MORD: But, Esther, remember that you, also, are a Jew. Your life will not be spared simply because you are queen. Besides, God may have made you queen to save all our lives! Please, Esther, no one else can plead for us, only you!

ESTHER: All right, Mordecai, I will plead with the king.

N 2: So Esther went to see the king.

N 1: She looked so sad and beautiful that the king raised his golden sceptre and called her to sit by him.

KING: What do you want, my dear? You can have anything you like.

N 2: Now, Esther had a plan in mind to save her people, the Jews.

ESTHER: Your Majesty, I would like you and Haman to have dinner with me tonight.

KING: Is that all, my dear?

ESTHER: Yes, Your Majesty.

KING: Then we would be delighted!

HAMAN: Dinner with the king and queen! Good!

N 2: At the meal, Esther asked them to come to dinner again the next evening.

N 1: But that night, the king couldn't sleep. He tossed and turned.

KING: Scribe! Bring the palace diary and read it to me!

SCRIBE: Your Majesty, there is a record here of one Mordecai, who saved Your Majesty's life by warning you of a plot to have you killed.

KING: Mordecai! Why, I had quite forgotten about him! I promised to reward him. Very well! Send for Haman, my Prime Minister, to give me advice.

SCRIBE: But, Your Majesty, it is the middle of the night!

KING: I don't care what time it is! Send for Haman now! I must reward Mordecai. He saved my life!

Ah, Haman, I need your advice! How would you reward a man to whom you were very grateful?

HAMAN: (*Aside.*) He must mean me. (*To the King.*) Why, Your Majesty, you should let him wear royal robes and give him the royal horse to ride. Let one of your highest officials lead him through the city. Let the official announce as they go, 'This is how the king honours a man!'

KING: Excellent! In the morning, send for Mordecai, give him my royal robes and my royal horse and you, Haman, shall lead the horse and do just what you have suggested.

N 2: Haman, as you can guess, was furious!

N 1: So he complained to his wife.

HAMAN: I hate Mordecai!

WIFE: Then do something about it! *You* are the Prime Minister!

HAMAN: I'll ask the king's permission to kill him – and I'll have the gallows built ready!

N 2: That night, Queen Esther looked more beautiful than ever.

KING: Esther, ask for anything you want and it will be granted.

ESTHER: Your Majesty, I am a Jew. We are a loyal people, who obey your laws. But a cruel man has decreed that we should all be killed.

KING: Who is this man?

ESTHER: It is Haman, your Prime Minister. He has even had a gallows built for Mordecai, who saved your life!

KING: Is this true, Haman?

HAMAN: Yes, Your Majesty!

KING: Then we shall use your gallows – to hang *you*! Take him away, guard! Now, I shall need a new Prime Minister. Send for Mordecai!

N 1: So Mordecai was made Prime Minister.

N 2: Esther had saved her people's lives.

N 1: God had made her queen for this very purpose.

N 2: And every year, the Jewish people celebrate Purim – the Festival of Lots – to celebrate…

N 1: … when God saved them from the cruel hand of Haman!

ASSEMBLY: ESTHER

THEME: *Bravery*

This play is based on the book of Esther.

You will need:

highlighter; sheet of paper headed 'Story Recipe for Esther' and felt-tip pens; sheet of paper headed 'Story Recipe for Cinderella', and on separate lines:

Cinderella, a poor servant girl
Loneliness
Two Ugly Sisters
Selfishness
A dance

Introduction

Class 3M enjoyed their gym lessons. They changed quickly, hurried into the hall and put out all the equipment. Mr Woodley checked it was all safe and then the lesson started. When it was Adrian's turn, he jumped high and straight off the horse, spreading out his arms just as he was told to. He landed well and Mr Woodley was pleased. Then it was Timothy's turn. He hated this! He scrambled up onto the horse, and looked over the side. He couldn't! He just couldn't do it! He climbed down again, and went to the back of the queue. Mr Woodley smiled at him, but said nothing. By the time it was his turn again, Timothy was determined to do it. He had spent weeks trying and it was time he did it, he thought. He climbed up, and stood straight – but that was too high! He crouched down, and very carefully jumped. He had done it! Mr Woodley clapped, and the others joined in. They knew what a struggle it had been for Timothy. But Adrian didn't clap. It had been a lousy jump – nothing like as good as his. It wasn't fair!

Core material

Why was Mr Woodley so pleased with Timothy? Bring out the fact that Timothy had overcome his fears. If someone isn't frightened, then they are not being brave in the same way as someone who is frightened. In the play, Esther was frightened. What didn't she want to do at first? She had good reason to be frightened of the king. Xerxes had got rid of his previous wife just because she wouldn't join him at a meal! If Esther went to see Xerxes when he hadn't sent for her, he could have her killed – and no one would try to stop him! No wonder she was frightened! Why did she agree to see the king, then? (Bring out the fact that she did it to help other people.)

We are going to write a 'Story Recipe' for the story we heard in the play. Explain this by showing them and completing the Story Recipe for the rest of Cinderella's story, beginning with the Fairy Godmother. Then write the recipe for the story of Esther. Point out that not just people and events are included in the Cinderella recipe, and ensure that such things as bravery, fear and the sceptre are included in the Esther one.

Prayer/Reflection

Highlight fear and bravery in the Story Recipe for Esther. Ask the pupils to look out for examples of others being brave during the next week, in and out of school.

OR

Highlight fear and bravery in the Story Recipe for Esther. Ask the pupils to think about these two things going together, and say this prayer as they listen: Thank you for the bravery of Esther. Help us to be brave as we face things which frighten us.

Music suggestions

- Be bold! Be strong!, 14, *Junior Praise*
- When the road, 279, *Junior Praise*

Background notes

- Shushan (Susa) was the winter residence of the king, Babylon his summer residence.
- See page 75 for notes on the Jews' exile in Babylon. The Persians allowed the Jews to return home if they wished, but by then some of the families were so settled that they opted to stay. Xerxes may be Ahasuerus, king of Persia, whose cruelty was noted by a Greek contemporary. Persian kings had many wives, only one bearing the title of queen at a time.
- Esther was queen – but she had no power, being utterly dependent on the king's goodwill.
- Mordecai refused to bow to Haman. Jews did bow to people as a mark of respect. Haman did not seem to have earned respect, so people were ordered to bow to him. Perhaps Mordecai knew that Haman would interpret a bow as a sign of worship – and Mordecai as a faithful Jew would not worship anyone but God.
- The Festival of Purim, celebrating Esther's bravery, is still held every year in Jewish families.
- The agreed signal that the king would listen to a suppliant was the raising of his golden sceptre, the symbol of his kingship.

NEW TESTAMENT PUPPET PLAYS

Puppet play: THE INNKEEPER'S STORY

CHARACTERS

INNKEEPER (INN)
HIS WIFE (WIFE)
MARY
JOSEPH (JOS)
SHEPHERD 1 (S 1)
SHEPHERD 2 (S 2)
WISE MEN (WM 1, WM 2, WM 3)

INN: I've been on my feet all day! They're killing me! All these visitors! In my little inn! I have to run around after them all. Hay for the donkeys! Straw for the asses! Water for the camels! Our little town wasn't built for so many people. Bethlehem's only a tiny little place! Tonight it's not just my inn that's full – it's everywhere! And all because the emperor, thousands of miles away in Rome, wants to know how many people there are in Israel – so he can raise the taxes, I've no doubt! So everyone has to go to the town where he was born. Everyone and his family! Bethlehem is full to overflowing. Jam-packed! There isn't a bed anywhere. Well, that's my lot! I'm off to have my supper. Then I'm going to fall into bed. I'll be up again at the crack of dawn. Another busy day! (*Knocking.*) Go away! (*More knocking.*) I said, 'Go away!' (*More knocking.*) We're full! Don't you understand? There's no room! (*More knocking.*)

WIFE: Aren't you going to answer the door, Malachi?

INN: Why is it always my job? Oh, very well! (*Opens door to Mary and Joseph.*) We're full up! No room! Got it?

JOS: I'm sorry to trouble you, sir, but we've come a long way…

INN: So's everyone else!

JOS: … and as you can see, sir, my wife will soon be giving birth.

INN: I've told you, we're full!

WIFE: Be quiet, man! Can't you see this young woman needs rest? Look, it isn't very comfortable, but there's a cave round the back where we keep the animals. It's not very special, but the hay is soft and the animals will keep you warm.

JOS: Thank you. (*They move to the cave.*)

WIFE: Here, settle yourself down, my dear.

MARY: You're very kind.

INN: And so it was that they came to my inn – a young woman, hardly more than a girl, and her husband. Quiet, honest folk. And I nearly turned them away! But it was here, in my inn, that the baby was born – well, in the cave, actually – in the middle of the night. They put the baby in a cattle-trough, full of hay. It was a boy! *Then* there were some strange goings on. I'd hardly dropped off to sleep when they arrived – shepherds! Shepherds from the hills!

S 1: Can we come in, sir, to see the baby?

JOS: Of course! But how did you know?

S 1: We saw angels! They were so bright, it fair blinded us! They told us to come to Bethlehem. They said we'd find a special baby. They said he was God's son. So we came – to worship!

S 2: And bring a gift. Here, this sheepskin will keep him warm.

INN: But that wasn't the end of it all! They stayed on for some time – the family. To look after the baby and give the girl time to rest they moved into a house nearby. That's when the other visitors arrived – I've never seen anything like it! One day they arrived, rich men they were, in fine clothes. They stopped and spoke to me, one by one.

WM 1: We are looking for a newborn king.

WM 2: We went to the royal palace in Jerusalem, thinking he would be there.

WM 3: But they directed us to Bethlehem – after much discussion!

WM 1: And here, sure enough, the star stopped!

WM 2: We have followed it for months…

WM 3: … over mountains and deserts, through forests and jungles, across rivers and seas, past cities and villages.

WM 1: The star has led us here.

INN: There is a child in the house just round here. I'll show you. (*Wise men kneel, one by one, in front of the baby.*)

WM 1: I bring a gift of gold for the King.

WM 2: I bring frankincense.

WM 3: I bring myrrh.

INN: There they knelt and worshipped the baby, then left as quickly as they came – their mission completed. But I noticed they left a different way – not back to Jerusalem. I wonder if they knew… Not long afterwards the family left, too. But not for Galilee where they came from. They went to Egypt.

JOS: God has warned me in a dream to take the child to safety.

INN: The baby, the star, the shepherds, the visitors from afar. Little Bethlehem had never known such things! But I'm glad we played our small part in the child's birth. And to think I almost turned them away!

ASSEMBLY: THE INNKEEPER'S STORY

THEME: *The first Christmas*

The Christmas story can be found in Matthew 1:18 – 2:18 and Luke 2:1–20.

Introduction

If the pupils were watching this play as a video, which three or four scenes do they think would be the most important? Decide on these, and then ask the puppeteers to reconstruct one (or two, depending on time) of them. Go through the characters involved in the scene. Ask for pupils to duplicate the scene in person. As each character takes up position, ask the others what s/he would be feeling at this stage in the story. When the scene is complete, ask the 'actors' if they think they can increase the drama of the scene by repositioning themselves, changing expressions, etc., in accordance with what was decided about their feelings. Ask them to make any changes they see fit. Concentrate on the feelings of the people involved. Thank both casts, and ask them to sit down.

Core material

We hear the Christmas story again and again. It is difficult to imagine just how amazing the events were to the people in the story. These were ordinary people, but extraordinary things happened to them. As we get ready for Christmas and then celebrate it, what feelings do we have? Are they all feelings that are nice to have? It wasn't like that for the people in the first Christmas. Many people were worried and frightened. Ask the pupils who felt like this and why. When we think about Jesus' birth, we imagine a nice warm and cosy stable, and Jesus lying in soft, warm hay. It wasn't like that. Mary and Joseph did the best they could, but they were in an animal shelter, probably a cave. It was cold and dark, and Mary must have been wishing she was at home, with her friends and family around her, and in a warm house with clean covers for her tiny baby. But God showed Mary and Joseph that he knew what was happening and that he was looking after them. For a long time, they had been the only ones who knew that Jesus was a special baby – the Son of God. Ever since the angel had come to Mary and told her about Jesus, they had kept their secret. But now God sent other people to share the news. He sent poor shepherds, people who everyone thought were unimportant. He sent rich important men from miles away. He used his own messengers, the angels, and a great star to guide these people. Mary and Joseph were reminded that this little baby, who seemed so ordinary, was very special indeed.

Prayer/Reflection

During this Christmas, think for a few minutes about that young couple who were trusted to look after God's Son. They were looking after God's gift to the world.

OR

Thank you, God, for sending Jesus to us as a helpless little baby – your gift to the world.

Music suggestions

- Come and join the celebration, 323, *Junior Praise*
- The shepherds were excited, 170, *Children's Praise*
- The Virgin Mary had a baby boy, 251, *Junior Praise*

Background notes

- Joseph was descended from King David who was from Bethlehem. So he and Mary had to travel there when the Roman Emperor ordered people to return to their family's home to be registered for taxation purposes. Bethlehem was small, and would probably not possess any real inns. Jewish homes were always open to those in need of lodging, though, because of their laws demanding hospitality.
- Many poor people shared their homes with their animals, living and sleeping on a small platform at one end of the only room. Others kept their animals in caves. The baby was put in a feeding trough, which would often have been a baby's first bed. Sometimes, a

hammock would be made from cloth stretched between two sticks stuck in the ground, or slung from a house's rafters. Newborn babies were rubbed with salt, believed to help their skin, and then wrapped tightly in strips of cloth over a large cloth. They believed this helped the limbs to grow straight and strong. It also gave the baby a feeling of security. The bands were loosened several times a day. Mary might have had the help of a local midwife.

- Hired shepherds were not highly thought of at the time. Their job was essential to Israel's economy, but they were not allowed to give testimony in court. The news of Jesus' birth was given to them first.
- There are several Herods in the New Testament. This one was known as Herod the Great. He rebuilt the temple, but was unpopular as he was the Romans' client king, and was not of pure Jewish descent. He actually killed some of his own children who had a better claim to the throne, so his action of killing the infants of Bethleham was not out of character. When the family returned from Egypt, Herod's son was king in Judea, so they settled in Galilee to avoid him.
- Gold was a mark of wealth, status and great worth, associated with worship in the temple. To Christians, it is a symbol of Christ's kingship. Frankincense and myrrh are both resins from shrubs, used as ingredients in the oil used to anoint priests. Frankincense was a sign that Jesus would act as a priest to his people, drawing them closer to God. Myrrh was associated with joy in the Old Testament, but was more usually used in the preparation of bodies for burial: it was a sign that Jesus was to die for his people. Christians believe that this death brought joy to them.

Puppet play: 'COME HOME, SON!'

CHARACTERS

NARRATOR (N)
FATHER (F)
FRIEND/S
POLICE OFFICER (PO)
YOUNGER SON (SON)
ELDER SON (ES)
PIG FARMER

N: There was once an old farmer who had two sons. The younger one was fed up with working on the farm.

SON: Boring!

N: He didn't want to become a farmer, so he asked his father for his share of the family wealth. The old man was sorry to see his son go, but he gave him his share and waved him goodbye. His son dashed off down the road.

SON: Mustn't miss my train! I'm off to the bright lights! London, here I come! I'll be a star!

N: In the big city, the son spent lots of money on expensive food...

SON: Delicious!

N: ... and wine...

SON: Cheers!

N: ... and friends...

SON: Yo!

N: Yes, he made a lot of friends – or did he? Then he ran out of money. He asked his friends for a loan.

SON: I say, old chap...

N: But they all turned him down.

FRIENDS: Sorry!

N: He had nowhere to live.

FRIENDS: Tough!

N: He was starving hungry!

SON: Rumble, rumble!

N: There were not many jobs around. At last, he got a job on a pig farm.

PIG FARMER: Slop out!

N: He slept in a cardboard box under the railway bridge.

SON: Cardboard city!

N: It was freezing at night. But the police kept moving them on.

PO: 'Ello, 'ello, 'ello, what have we got 'ere?

N: Then he had a brilliant idea!

SON: I'll go home. I'll work on Dad's farm. I don't deserve to be his son any more. I'll be a servant. Good food! A warm bed under a dry roof!

N: So he began to walk home. Soon his legs ached and his feet were blistered.

SON: My feet are killing me!

N: But what about his father? All this time, he had been worrying about his younger son. Then he saw a figure coming down the lane. It was his son!

SON: Sorry!

N: The father ran down the lane and shook his son's hand.

FATHER: Welcome home, son!

N: His father threw a party for his son.

FATHER: Meat pie! Coke! Disco!

N: His son, who he loved, had come home safe and sound.

FATHER: He's alive! We'll have a right good knees-up!

[*The play can finish at this point for younger pupils.*]

N: Ah, but there were two sons, weren't there? Now, the elder brother was just getting home from a hard day's work in the fields. He was tired out!

ES: Aah!

N: The party was just getting into full swing. The elder brother saw his younger brother, and realised what the party was for.

ES: What a cheek!

N: He was so angry that he went upstairs and sulked. His father tried to explain that he wasn't treating his younger son as a favourite.

FATHER: I love you both the same! But I had lost your brother – and he has come home to me!

N: But his elder son just went on sulking!

ASSEMBLY: 'COME HOME, SON!'

THEME: *God's forgiveness*

This play is based on the parable of the lost son, which can be found in Luke 15:11–32.

You will need:

paper chains to link pupils, eg the gummed strips used for Christmas decorations (If these are unavailable, strips of paper can be sticky taped together), one link with 'I'm sorry' on one side, and 'I forgive' you on the other side.

Introduction

Choose two pupils. Fasten a paper strip around one wrist of each pupil. Explain that these two are friends, and that friends are linked by 'chains' of liking and shared feelings. Link the two together with one or two more strips. But sometimes one of them will do something that hurts and upsets the other one, and the friendship 'chain' is broken. Ask the pupils to snap the chain by pulling apart. The friendship can be mended, though. Ask them how. When saying sorry is mentioned, show them the link with this written on. Point out that it has something else written on it, and read it to them. What does this mean? Discuss the meaning of forgiveness. If we forgive someone, we do not think again about what they did wrong. We forget it, and we let them forget about it too. If we don't, the friendship will never be the same again. Fasten this strip to the others, so that the friendship 'chain' is complete again. Of course, it is no good saying 'Sorry' or 'I forgive you' unless we really mean it. The friendship will not be mended if we are just pretending. Thank the pupils, unattach them, and ask them to sit down again.

Core material

In the play, someone spoiled a friendship or a relationship. Ask the pupils these questions: Who was it? What did he do? When he returned home and said, 'Sorry', what did his father do? What would have happened if his father had said, 'You did wrong, and I never want to see you again'? Would the relationship have been mended?
(If you used the second ending, about the elder brother, add: What about the elder brother? Did he forgive his brother? Do you think that he was happy at the end? Would his father and brother be happy when they thought about him? What could he do to make everyone happy again?)

This play is based on one of the parables Jesus told. (See and use as necessary the explanation about parables on page 33.) The father in the story is a picture of God. Ask if the father wanted his son to come home. He knew that his son had to come by himself – he had to want to say sorry. But the father was waiting for him. He was ready to forgive his son as soon as he came. He didn't expect him to say sorry over and over again. He didn't want him to work hard to give him the money back. All he wanted was to forgive his son, and he did this as soon as he said he was sorry. Jesus was saying that this is what God is like. He is waiting for people to come to him and to say sorry for wrong things they have done. As soon as they say this and really mean it, he forgives them – whatever they have done. Christians believe that God is like this, and that he will forgive people when they say sorry.

Prayer/Reflection

Help us, Father, to know when we have upset people, and to say sorry and really mean it . Help us, too, to forgive people who are sorry they have hurt us.

Music suggestions

- Children of God, 137, *A Year of Celebration*
- If you climb, 388, *Junior Praise*
- I look out through the doorway, 371, *Junior Praise*; 80, *Children's Praise*

Background notes

- A son leaving home like this would have brought shame on the whole family.

- The elder brother had every right to be angry: his brother had wasted a large part of the family security.
- The lost son was desperate indeed to take a job feeding pigs as they were an unclean animal to the Jews. Even touching them was forbidden in the Law.
- The son comes home with less than honourable intentions: he wants to be fed and clothed again. But the father welcomes him back unconditionally. The ring is a sign of the son's family authority, the sandals are a symbol of sonship and the clothes are a mark of honour. Everyone could see that he had been fully reinstated. Christians believe that they are accepted into God's family with the full rights and privileges of 'sons': it is as if they, too, receive the ring of sonship.

Puppet play: ROCKY ROAD AND SANDY LANE

CHARACTERS

NARRATOR (N)
ALBERT
MABEL
FRED SOLID
SID
DOLORES
BUILDER
RADIO

N: There was once a man…

ALBERT: Hello, my name's Albert Wise, and this is my wife, Mabel.

MABEL: Pleased to meet you.

N: They wanted to build a new house. But *where* should they build it?

MABEL It's lovely down by the river, Albert. Lovely and flat in Sandy Lane!

ALBERT: You don't want to build there, Mabel. It's all sandy! Just think what would happen if we had a lot of rain. We'd have a flood, wouldn't we? And then what would happen? The house would be swept away! No. We need some nice strong rock to build on. Look, that's the place for us, up on Rocky Road. If we ever get a flood we'll be as safe as houses there. As safe as houses! It's a joke! Get it?

MABEL Oh, all right, Albert, Rocky Road it is!

N: At the same time, another man, Mr Sid Flash, decided to build a house.

DOLORES: Oh, I've just seen a beautiful place for our dream house, darling! On Sandy Lane. It's nice and flat with a lovely view of the river.

SID: Oh, good! The builders will soon get the job done if it's sandy, darling. Sandy Lane it is!

DOLORES: And the builders can put in a swimming pool while they're at it.

SID: Yes, darling!

DOLORES: And a jacuzzi.

SID: Yes, darling!

DOLORES: And a spa bath.

SID: Yes, darling!

DOLORES: Oh, don't forget the satellite dish, darling!

SID: No, darling!

N: The builders soon got to work on the two houses. The one on Sandy Lane was finished in no time.

BUILDER: There we are, Mr Flash! Beautiful job!

SID: You were quick!

BUILDER: Well, it was a doddle, building on sand. Look at old Fred Solid over there building on that rock. It'll take him ages to finish that house!

N: But Fred Solid wasn't bothered. He liked to do a really solid job. (*We see Fred Solid building the house.*)

FRED: It'll be a while yet, Mr Wise, before we finish. But it'll be worth waiting for. This house'll be as solid as rock – after all, that's what it's built on – solid rock! Get it? Solid rock! Ha-ha-ha!

N: Sid and Dolores Flash moved into their new home in Sandy Lane.

SID: Coming to try out the swimming pool, Dolores?

DOLORES: When I've had a jacuzzi, darling. And a spa bath! Can you tune in the TV?

N: It was some time later when Albert and Mabel Wise finally moved into Rocky Road.

MABEL Ooooh, this is really cosy, Albert!

ALBERT: Yes, we'll be as safe as houses here, Mabel! Ha-ha-ha!

MABEL Hello, looks like rain, Albert!

ALBERT: Yes, I don't like the look of those black clouds, Mabel.

RADIO: The Met Office has just issued a warning of severe weather in the river area. Torrential rain is forecast with the danger of major flooding.

MABEL Oooh! Look at that rain, Albert!

ALBERT: Don't worry, Mabel, we're safe here on Rocky Road.

MABEL Look at those floods, Albert! I'm glad we didn't build on the sand down by the river. There's lots of wood being washed away in the flood.

ALBERT: Yes, looks as if some poor soul's house has had it! (*Knock on door.*)

MABEL I'd better see who that is. (*Sid and Dolores appear, looking very bedraggled.*)

SID AND DOLORES: Help!

MABEL You look soaked! You'd better come in and get dry by the fire. Albert, put the kettle on! You live in that new house on Sandy Lane, don't you?

SID: We did! Until a few minutes ago!

DOLORES: Then the floods came.

SID: And swept our lovely new house away!

ALBERT: I told you we'd be glad we built on Rocky Road, didn't I, Mabel? Always build on the… rock!

Assembly: ROCKY ROAD AND SANDY LANE

THEME: *Building our lives*
This play is based on the parable of the two builders which can be found in Luke 6:46–49.

You will need:
building blocks, enough to build two 'houses'; two sheets of paper or small boards to act as roofs; two trays, one with a layer of safe clean sand and one empty; a plastic jug filled with water; labels and Blu-Tack*; felt-tip pens*

Introduction

Choose two teams of pupils and ask each one to build one of the two houses mentioned in the play. One team is to use the empty tray, the other is to build on the sand in the other tray. When the houses are completed, ask the others what happened next. Pour the water on the sand around the house (you may need to jiggle the tray a little!). Do the same to the other house. Ask why the house on the sand collapsed. (If there are any building sites nearby, the foundations there can be discussed at this point.) So this is a story telling us how we should build houses – but few of us ever have a chance to choose a site and build a house. Jesus meant his listeners to learn something else from this story.

Core material

For many hundreds of years, Jewish writers had been calling God 'the Rock'. Listen to these verses from the Bible: 'The Lord is the everlasting rock', Isaiah 26:4; 'God is the rock and everything he does is perfect', Deuteronomy 32:4; 'The Lord is my rock and my safe place', Psalm 18:2 – and there are many others. So when Jesus talked about a rock, his listeners might think about God. He was telling them to build their lives upon him, and not upon other things that would not be safe and strong. What does it mean – to build your life upon something? Jesus meant that they should make him the most important thing in their lives. They should try to do as he wanted them to do. They should fill their lives with the sort of things he would choose, such as helping others, listening to his teaching, being kind. If they tried to follow him, then they would be building their lives on him and on his teaching. Write 'Jesus – the Rock' on one of the labels, and attach it to the inside base of the empty tray. Ask the pupils to tell you some of the things that a life built on Jesus would be made up of – such as kindness, helping others, listening to God – and write each one on a label, attaching it to a brick of the house built on the 'rock'. Then ask for the opposites of these where possible, and attach these to the fallen bricks of the other house. What is this life built on? Some people build their lives on things like money, or power, or learning. Can they think of others? 'Label' the sand with these things. So we know now what the sand and the rock and the houses stood for. But what about the storm? Talk about how we feel in a severe storm – especially at the seaside. It seems that the waves are going to overwhelm us, and that the wind will blow us over. Sometimes we feel as if we are in a storm in life. Things go wrong, sad things happen. Ask the pupils for examples of these, being sensitive to any who might feel they are in a 'storm' at the moment. Label the jug of water with these things. These are the things which threaten to defeat us and destroy our lives. But Jesus said that if we have built our lives on a firm, strong foundation, we will be safe.

Prayer

Thank you, Jesus, that you are as strong and safe as a great rock. When the storms of life are too strong for us, you are always there to help us.

Music suggestions

- Jesus is the rock, 170, *A Year of Celebration*
- The building song, 61, *The Complete Come and Praise*
- Don't build your house, 39, *Junior Praise*

Background notes

- Jesus was saying it is not enough to hear his words: they must be put into practice as well.
- There is a lot of sandy soil in Palestine. The houses were made of mud bricks, baked hard by the sun, so flooding was particularly hazardous, and flash floods were common.

Puppet play: THE SOWER AND THE SEEDS

CHARACTERS

NARRATOR 1 (N 1)	SEED 1	DAD
NARRATOR 2 (N 2)	SEED 2	TEACHER (T)
LADY	SEED 3	GRANDMA (G)
VICAR	SEED 4	GIRL
DAVID	SEED 5	MUM
DAVID'S WIFE (WIFE)	SEED 6	BIRD

N 1: * A farmer went out to sow, and as he scattered the seeds, some fell along the path…

SEED 1: Ooooh!

SEED 2: Ouch! Ooooh!

SEED 1: This path is hard!

N 1: * And the birds came and ate them up.

SEED 2: Look out! Birds!

SEED 1: Maybe they're not hungry.

SEED 2: They're always hungry!

SEED 1: That one's seen us! Duck!

SEED 2: It was nice knowing you!

SEED 1: Aaaargh!

SEED 2: Aaaargh!

BIRD: M-m-m-m! Delicious!

N 2: Great story, but what was it all about?

N 1: + Funny you should ask that, because Jesus had to explain it when he first told it. He said that the seeds which fell on the stony path were like someone who hears what is said, but doesn't understand it, and the devil won't let him take it in.

(*Enter Vicar and lady.*)

LADY: Lovely sermon, Vicar!

VICAR: Thank you, Mrs Brown. But which part did you like best?

LADY: Oh, er, I'm not sure, er, I must ask you what it was all about some time. Anyway, I've got to be off now – my old man'll want his roast beef and Yorkshire pudding! Then there's the ironing. Bye, Vicar! Thank you!

VICAR: I don't think she understood at all.

N 1: * But that's not all! Some seeds fell on rocky ground, where there wasn't much soil, and straight away they sprang up.

SEEDS: Boing!

SEED 3: Great!

SEED 4: Super! All we have to do now is lie here and let the sun do all the work for us!

N 1: * But when the sun got up, the seeds were scorched.

SEED 3: I say, got anything to drink, old chap?

SEED 4: Sorry, old thing! Solid rock under here!

SEED 3: I'm coming over all faint…

SEED 4: I'm shrivelling up!

SEED 3: (*Cough.*)

SEED 4: (*Cough.*)

SEED 3: It was nice knowing you…

SEED 4: (*Cough.*)

N 1: + Yes, some people have got no staying power. They shoot up like those seeds with no roots – and they give up easily, too!

GIRL: My name's Cynthia. I pwomised my Sunday School Teacher I'd help evewywone I met this week.

MUM: Cynthia, you promised you'd wash the pots!

DAD: You told your little sister you'd take her swimming.

T: Cynthia, you promised you'd collect up the Maths books!

G: You said you'd weed my garden because I've got a bad back, Cynthia!

N 1: Did she keep all her promises? Tut-tut-tut! You promised! (*Wags finger at Cynthia who bursts into tears and runs off.*)

N 1: ⋆ Now, some seeds fell among thorns…

SEED 5: Ouch!

SEED 6: Oooh!

N 1: ⋆ They grew a bit, but then the thorns grew up and choked them! (*Enter bully-boy thorn.*)

SEED 5: Look out! It's the Thorn!

SEED 6: Too late! (*Thorn drags them off-stage, still crying.*)

N 1: + Nasty! They're like people who hear God's word, but are too busy to do anything about it.

(*This scene has two parts to the stage: right and left, to represent the two ends of a telephone conversation.*)

VICAR: Hello, David, any chance of you cutting old Mrs Smith's lawn for her?

DAVID: Sorry, Vicar, I'm mending the vacuum cleaner. Then I've got to go to work. Really sorry, Vicar! See you! (*Puts down phone.*) That got rid of him!

WIFE: Tom says he'll see you at the pub later on for the darts match.

DAVID: Great! Fancy a video when I get in?

N 1: + ⋆ He was too busy. What a pity! Still, some people do hear what God is saying to them *and* put it into action! Jesus said, 'Other seeds fell on good soil and brought forth a really good crop: some a hundredfold; some sixty; and some thirty.'

ASSEMBLY: THE SOWER AND THE SEEDS

THEME: *Learning*

This play is based on the parable of the sower which can be found in Luke 8:1–15.

You will need:

two sheets of paper; felt-tip pens

Introduction

This play is different from the others about Jesus' parables, because this one tells us the story Jesus told as well as putting that story into a modern setting. Read out the speeches marked *: these are Jesus' original story. Jesus did most of his teaching in the open air, in the villages, and in the fields and hills around them. It is easy to imagine him looking round as he told this story, and watching a sower as he worked on the land. Jesus' listeners would have understood what was happening to the seeds immediately: many of them had the same problems as this sower! But they were probably as puzzled as we are when they thought about what the story could mean. Jesus' disciples were so confused that they asked him to explain the story's meaning to them afterwards. This is what he said. Read out the speeches marked * again, but slot in Jesus' explanations, marked +: (Some words will need omitting for sense.) But it is still hard to understand! The modern passages help us in this.

Core material

This parable is about what people do when they hear Jesus' teaching. If they are to learn about God and put what they learn into practice and live as God wants them to do, then they need certain conditions – just as the seeds need certain conditions to grow. In fact, all people need certain conditions before they can learn anything properly. Ask the pupils to help you make a list of the conditions seeds need to grow, using what they have heard in the play, and what they know from other sources. On the other sheet of paper, build up a list of the conditions people need to learn effectively. This should include their own ideas as well as ideas they have gained from the play. For instance, they could include being comfortable so they can concentrate; having no distractions; having an interesting teacher. Conclude that people cannot learn anything properly – about God or about anything – if they do not have the right conditions, including things like these.

Did anyone mention having an example to follow? If someone is teaching us how to do things, one of the most helpful ways of doing this is to show us how to do it. Add this to the list if necessary. Christians believe that Jesus did not just tell people how God wanted them to live, he also showed them how to live this way as he travelled round their towns and villages, caring for people and looking after them. They also believe that he showed people what God was like.

Prayer/Reflection

When we begin to learn something new, it is easy to become discouraged, and to think that we will never manage it. Are you thinking this about something at the moment? We have to be patient with ourselves, and keep on trying, and we should always ask for help when we need it. At the same time, we should be careful that we are not making it harder for someone else to learn anything.

OR

Thank you, Father, that Jesus spent time teaching about you and your love for us, showing people how to live and also showing them what you are like. Help us as we learn more about you and the world. Thank you that we have the freedom to learn about so many things, and the conditions in which we can do this.

Music suggestions

God has given me his word, 37, *Children's Praise*

It's a happy day, 118, *Junior Praise*

Background notes

- This is the nearest thing to an allegory out of the parables in this book. Each part represents something else.
- Most of the land in Palestine is not very fertile. Stones, shallow soil, birds and weeds were constant problems for many of Jesus' listeners.

NOTES

by John Webster

I have found the children's shelves of my local library to be a great source of new ideas for simple puppets to make easily and quickly with children.

Highly recommended to me is a book on Christian puppetry published by Marshall Pickering: *Puppets in Praise* by Stuart Holt.

Finally, I'm always willing to try to help and encourage you with your puppetry and drama. My telephone number is 0115 9160920.

BIBLIOGRAPHY FOR SIMPLE PUPPETS TO MAKE IN THE CLASSROOM

Children's books:

D Robson and V Bailey, *Rainy Day Puppets*, Franklyn Watts, 1990, ISBN 0 74960 219 8

T Smith, *Finger Puppet Fun*, Lorenz Books, 1996 ISBN 1 85967 321 X

K Haines and G Harvey, The Usborne Book of Puppets, Usborne Books, 1997, ISBN 0 74602 724 9

M Doney, World Crafts Puppets, Watts Books, 1995, ISBN 0 74961 941 4

Adult books:

R Humbert, *Puppets and Marionettes*, Magnet Books, 1988, ISBN 0 41612 922 6

J Gammon, Easy to Make Puppets, Anaya Publishers, 1993, ISBN 1 85470 042 1

INDEX OF BIBLICAL PEOPLE AND STORIES

Abednego		69,71
Centurion		58
Daniel		69,71
David		16
Elisha		19
Esther		75
Fiery furnace		69
Goliath		16
Jacob		11
Jesus		28,31,53,56,58,61,80
– and see under parables		
John		58,61
Jonah		23
Joseph		11
Joseph, Mary's husband		80
Lions' den		71
Mary		58,80
Mary Magdalene		61
Meshach		69
Naaman		19
Parables	Good Samaritan	47
	Lost sheep	44
	Lost son	84
	Rich fool	39
	Sower	91
	Talents	51
	Two houses	88
	Two sons	34
	Unforgiving servant	36
	Wedding feast	42
Peter		53,56,61
Saul		16
Shadrach		69
Shem		8
Zacchaeus		28

THEMATIC INDEX

This is not intended to be an exhaustive list of the themes contained in the biblical material used, but is intended as a guide to facilitate the matching of the text to syllabuses. The theme of each story which is explored in its assembly is listed in ordinary type: other themes which the teacher could use the play to explore are listed in italics.

Bravery	75,*56,69,71*
Building lives	88
Change	*11,19*
Cost of giving	*31*
Cost of helping	*47*
Christmas	80
Failure	56
Fear	*56*
Feelings	*56*
Forgiving others	*11,23,36,84*
Giving	31,*47*
God's care for everybody	44
God's forgiveness	84,*23,28,36*
God's invitation	42
God's help	*16*
God's love	28,*23*
God's omnipresence	*23*
God's perfect planning	11,*75*
God's universal mercy	23
God's word	*91*
Healing	*19*
Helping each other	*19*
Jealousy	*11*
Jesus' death	58
Jesus' forgiveness	56,*28*
Jesus' love	*44*
Jesus' resurrection	61
Judging others	*36*
Kingship of Jesus	53
Learning	91
Loyalty	*69,71*
Motivation	*31*
Neighbours	47
Obedience	8,*34*
Opposites	*16*
Our talents	51
Pride	*19*
Priorities	39,*28,42*
Real giving	31
Real wealth	*28,39*
Reconciliation	*11*
Saying sorry	*28,84*
Self-sacrifice	*44*
Sharing	*34*
Standing up for beliefs	*69*,71
Surprises	*61*
Treating others as we treat ourselves	36
Trust in God	16,*8,31,69*
Witnesses of God	69,*71*
Words and actions	34,*58,88*

Other resources from Scripture Union

Everyone Matters: Outlines for Junior Assemblies
Tricia Williams

Over forty outlines for creating lively and interesting assemblies suitable for Key Stage 2 pupils.

Each outline is Bible based and has been tested by the contributors. There is a variety of presentation methods, some using interactive participation. All outlines are carefully structured and clearly set out for easy use by busy teachers.

ISBN 1 85999 040 1
£6.99

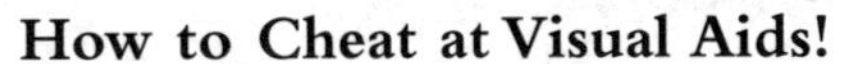

How to Cheat at Visual Aids!
People remember 30% of what they hear, but 60% of what they see and hear – that makes this guide to producing visual aids indispensable. Over 500 pictures of New Testament characters and stories.
PHOTOCOPIABLE
ISBN 0 86201 990 7
£6.99

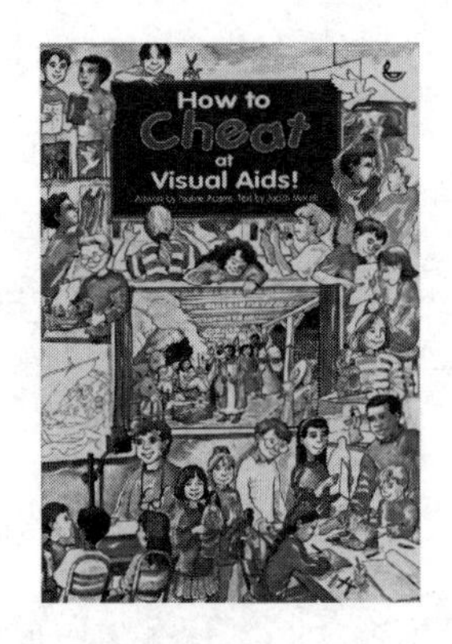

How to Cheat at Visual Aids! Old Testament
A follow-on from the well-received How to Cheat at Visual Aids, this volume deals specifically with Old Testament people, events and festivals. May be used with the original How to Cheat... or alone.
PHOTOCOPIABLE
ISBN 1 85999 161 0
£7.99

Maximus Mouse
Brian Ogden

Maximus is a lively and determined mouse who lives in St Michael's Church. He listens to the Sunday talks on The Lord's Prayer and has some amusing misunderstandings on the way to getting the real point. Fifteen short stories which have proved immensely popular for junior assemblies.

ISBN 0 86201 680 0
£3.25

Other titles in the Maximus series
Each book contains short stories about Maximus and his friends which are amusing and also carry an important teaching point.

Maximus Rides Again
ISBN 0 86201 834 X
£2.99

Maximus and the Great Expedition
ISBN 0 86201 9
£3.25

Maximus and the Computer Mouse
ISBN 1 85999 181 5
£3.50